D1477793

PAUL GRAY
DEBORAH JUMP
HANNAH SMITHSON

ADVERSE CHILDHOOD EXPERIENCES AND SERIOUS YOUTH VIOLENCE

BRISTOL
UNIVERSITY
PRESS

First published in Great Britain in 2023 by

Bristol University Press
University of Bristol
1-9 Old Park Hill
Bristol
BS2 8BB
UK
t: +44 (0)117 374 6645
e: bup-info@bristol.ac.uk

Details of international sales and distribution partners are available at
bristoluniversitypress.co.uk

British Library Cataloguing in Publication Data
A catalogue record for this book is available from the British Library

ISBN 978-1-5292-2593-8 hardcover
ISBN 978-1-5292-2594-5 ePub
ISBN 978-1-5292-2595-2 ePdf

Cover design: blu inc
Front cover image: gettyimages/Slonov
Bristol University Press uses environmentally responsible
print partners.
Printed in Great Britain by CPI Group (UK) Ltd,
Croydon, CR0 4YY

FSC
www.fsc.org
MIX
Paper | Supporting
responsible forestry
FSC® C013604

Contents

List of Figures and Tables iv

Acknowledgements v

one   Introduction   1

two   Review of the Literature   9

three   Researching Adverse Childhood   21
        Experiences and Trauma

four   Serious Youth Violence   41

five   Adverse Childhood Experiences   54

six   The Relationship between Adverse   69
        Childhood Experiences and Serious
        Youth Violence

seven   Trauma-informed Practice   84

eight   Conclusions   100

Notes   106

References   110

Index   126

List of Figures and Tables

Figures

2.1	Types of ACEs	14
3.1	The ACEs assessment tool	23
3.2	Story 1 – Jack and Paul	36
3.3	Story 2 – Joe's kidnap	37
4.1	Excerpt from Story 1	52
5.1	Number of ACEs	55
5.2	Types of ACEs	59
5.3	Excerpt from Story 2	67

Tables

3.1	Comparison of all open cases and ACEs assessment cases	26
3.2	Narrative interview participants	30
3.3	Workshop 1 participants	33
3.4	Workshop 2 participants	33
3.5	The main reasons for young people's involvement in violence	39
3.6	During an act of violence young people are thinking	39
3.7	What ACEs have young people who have been involved in violence had?	39
3.8	Types of support needed by young people	39
3.9	Who needs to offer the support?	40

Acknowledgements

The research on which this book is based was commissioned by Marie McLaughlin, Head of Manchester Youth Justice, and funded by the Youth Justice Board's *Reducing Serious Youth Violence (Reference Group) Pathfinder* programme. The authors would like to thank all those who gave up their time to be involved in the research. This includes: the twelve youth justice workers and nine justice-involved young people that agreed to be interviewed; the seven justice-involved young people that participated in the participatory workshops; the three therapists from One Education in Manchester – Deirdre McConnell, James Stephens and Kate Brown – who delivered the creative workshops; Rob Jones from Manchester Metropolitan University who delivered the sports-based elements of the workshops; and Lucy Perrone from Manchester Youth Justice who provided the quantitative data on all open cases during the research period. The authors would like to give a special thanks to Thomas Lang at Manchester Youth Justice. His commitment to the research and the time he gave to help facilitate the delivery of the various elements was invaluable.

ONE

Introduction

Background to the research

The city of Manchester in the northwest of England has a rich history. The industrial revolution resulted in it becoming the world's first industrialized city. It was the birthplace of the suffragette movement and globally it is recognized for its substantial contributions to culture, sport and music. However, Manchester could be described as a 'tale of two cities'. For instance, while economic growth in the city in 2021 was the second highest out of 30 major European cities (Avison Young 2022), according to the 2019 Index of Multiple Deprivation,[1] Manchester ranked as the sixth most deprived local authority in England (Ministry of Housing, Communities and Local Government 2019). Indeed, at the start of 2022, around one in four young people in the city were living in poverty (Greater Manchester Poverty Action 2022). While the relationship between poverty and childhood adversity is complicated, living in persistent poverty remains (at the neighbourhood level) a key predictor of youth offending (Jahanshahi et al 2022).

When it comes to youth offending in Manchester, 'serious youth violence' (hereafter referred to as SYV) – defined as 'any drug, robbery or violence against the person offence that has a gravity score of five of more'[2] (Home Office 2018) – rose by over 200 per cent between 2016/17 and 2018/19. And in 2018/19, Manchester had the highest rate of SYV offences[3] out of all the youth justice services across England and Wales that were included in the Youth Justice Board's Serious Youth Violence Reference Group.[4] Indeed, a fifth of all youth offences in Manchester during

2018/19 were classed as SYV. This high prevalence of serious violence has been reflected in media headlines over the last few years, and a perusal of *Manchester Evening News* headlines since the start of 2021 reveals a range of SYV offences.[5] As can be seen in the sample of headlines that follows, in media discourse the term SYV is often used interchangeably with other evocative terms such as knife crime or youth gangs:

- The violent teenage gang feud being fought with axes and machetes on the streets of Oldham (13 March 2021)
- Boy, 14, 'stabbed in stomach and arm' during horror assault prompting 15 arrests for 'serious youth violence' (19 August 2021)
- Children killing children: Inside Greater Manchester's teen knife crime epidemic (30 January 2022)

Notwithstanding these febrile media headlines, it is important to note that SYV is not simply a Manchester problem. Although the Crime Survey for England and Wales (CSEW) shows that levels of interpersonal violence have been steadily declining since the mid-1990s (Billingham and Irwin-Rogers 2022),[6] SYV is a growing concern across England and Wales. This is largely a result of year-on-year increases in knife and offensive weapon offences involving those aged 10–17 years. For example, in 2013 2,639 young people were charged with these types of offence. By 2019 this had risen to 4,562 (Ministry of Justice 2020), and in 2020 248 people were stabbed to death in England and Wales (Home Office 2022). Alongside this, it has been found that both perpetrators and victims of SYV offences are getting younger, with self-reported violence peaking at age 15 (Home Office 2018). When it comes to the cost of SYV, it was estimated that in 2018/19 SYV in England and Wales had a total economic and social cost of £1.3 billion; a rise of over 50 per cent from 2014/15 (Irwin-Rogers et al 2020).

The rise in SYV and the associated economic and societal cost has served to increase political and populist concerns around SYV, resulting in a raft of new laws, policies and initiatives to tackle the issue. For example, in 2016 the cross-party Youth Violence Commission was established, delivering its final report in 2020 (Irwin-Rogers et al 2020). The year 2018 saw the cross-party Serious Violence Taskforce established that resulted in the Home Office's Serious Violence Strategy (Home Office 2018). In 2019, the UK's prime minister convened an emergency 'Serious Violence Summit' and, in the same year, dedicated Violence Reduction Units were introduced in areas worst affected by violent crime (Home Office 2020). Vast sums of government monies have been allocated to address SYV including, for example, an initial £35 million for the Violence Reduction Units and £200 million to the ten-year Youth Endowment Fund.[7] At a legislative level, Knife Crime Prevention Orders have been rolled out across police forces in England and Wales. The stated aim of these Orders is to prevent young people aged 12 and over from carrying knives and becoming involved in serious violence (Home Office 2021).[8]

Concomitant with these political responses to SYV is the growing body of research that has identified the disproportionate prevalence of 'adverse childhood experiences' (hereafter referred to as ACEs) among justice-involved young people; particularly those who perpetrate violent offences. ACEs commonly describe ten specific types of abuse, neglect and/or household dysfunction. Since the mid-1990s, research (Boswell 1996; Jacobson et al 2010; Martin et al 2021) has consistently shown that young people entering the justice system are much more likely to have experienced ACEs than those in the general population. Yet despite this, it is only in the last few years that ACEs have become part of the 'mainstream conversation' about SYV (Irwin-Rogers et al 2020: 76). This is surprising when one considers that ACEs have been shown to increase the risk of a young person perpetrating a violent offence (Fox et al 2015), with each additional ACE increasing the risk by between 35 per cent and 144 per cent (Duke et al 2010). Indeed, the more ACEs a young person has, the greater the possibility of them being classified as a serious violent offender (Perez et al 2018).

While it might appear obvious that there is some form of relationship between ACEs and SYV, there is a striking dearth of research that has investigated this relationship in any detail. By using Manchester as a case study, the research on which this book is based directly addresses this lack of knowledge and understanding. It is worth noting at the outset that the aim of the research was not to conduct a comprehensive investigation into the biopsychosocial explanations for SYV. Rather, the explicit focus was the under-researched relationship between ACEs and SYV. This research brought together an innovative mix of methods, including a bespoke quantitative tool designed by the research team to assess ACEs, qualitative interviews with youth justice workers and narrative life-story interviews with justice-involved young people. Crucially, the research also included a series of participatory creative workshops involving drama therapists, a professional sports coach and justice-involved young people. Unlike in other contexts (such as health care) that have a more established track-record of service user co-production and participation (Beckett et al 2018), young people in a justice context are rarely given the opportunity to inform policy and service provision; their status as 'young offenders' often precludes their participation (Byrne and Lundy 2019). As members of the award-winning Manchester Centre for Youth Studies[9] – a research centre that prides itself on delivering youth-informed and youth-led research – it was important to us that justice-involved young people and their voices would be central to the research.

This innovative methodology was necessary because as a team we wanted to (quantitatively) identify the nature and prevalence of ACEs among justice-involved young people in Manchester, as well as centre the voices of those who are not usually heard. Thus, we aimed to (qualitatively) explore young people's own articulations of the causes and drivers of SYV. Through this exploration, we were able to develop a deeper, more detailed understanding of the relationship between ACEs and SYV and make recommendations that consider the views and experiences of justice-involved young people. Our overall aim was to adopt a psychotherapeutically informed approach that would enable us to move beyond current criminological and socio-political perspectives that all too often characterize perpetrators of SYV as either rationally acting thrill-seekers or pathologically evil 'monsters' that require harsh punishment. By adopting such an approach, this book builds on our earlier work (Gray 2008; 2010; 2015; Jump 2014; 2020; Jump and Smithson 2020) and starts to theoretically unpick why SYV might seem appealing or even necessary to those young people who perpetrate it. Furthermore, it looks at how the approach we have adopted might usefully inform youth justice policy and practice when it comes to working effectively with young perpetrators of serious violence. While there is a growing acknowledgement within the youth justice sector of the need to be trauma-informed (Liddle et al 2016; Cordis Bright 2017; Glendinning et al 2021) and an associated proliferation of trauma-informed approaches, there remains a lack of inquiry into the evidence base for and efficacy of such approaches. To address this gap in knowledge, our research also explored both young people's and youth justice workers' experiences of trauma-informed practice, and discussed the value that a more psychotherapeutically informed approach might add to existing ways of working.

Structure of the book

Chapter 2 engages with the literature around the four main topics covered in this book: SYV, ACEs, trauma-informed practice and participatory practice. The chapter starts with a section that looks at the causes and consequences of SYV, before moving on to outline and critique the political response to SYV in England and Wales. This is followed by a section on ACEs that summarizes the body of largely quantitative and retrospective research that has followed the original ACEs study by Felitti et al (1998). It analyses the academic literature around the nature and prevalence of ACEs among justice-involved young people, and the wide-ranging impact that ACEs can have on a young person. This leads on to a discussion of the physical and psychological impact of ACEs, and the need for a trauma-informed approach when working with justice-involved young people who have experienced adversity. The final section in this chapter addresses the growing emphasis on participatory practice with justice-involved young people that was first advocated in the mid-2010s. It engages with the debates around young people's rights to participation, along with a discussion of the benefits and challenges of implementing meaningful participation in a youth justice context.

Chapter 3 covers the various methodological approaches that were utilized in this research. The quantitative, qualitative and participatory methodologies that were adopted and the rationale for using them are each discussed. The first section introduces the bespoke ACEs assessment tool that was developed for the research, along with a discussion of how and why it was delivered, and why the tool was completed by youth justice workers rather than self-completed by young people. This is followed by description of how the research team trained a sample of youth justice workers to undertake narrative interviews with the young people on their caseload using the McAdams Life Story Approach (Bauer and McAdams 2004). The final section in the chapter details the approach that was adopted to undertake the participatory creative workshops with justice-involved young people. The workshops, delivered in partnership with creative therapists and a professional sports coach, used Dent-Brown and Wang's (2006) 6-Part Story Method to elicit data from the young people. The chapter finishes with a visual depiction of the six-part stories that were created during the participatory workshops, along with the themes that emerged from the workshops.

Chapter 4 is the first of four chapters that present the findings from the research. It starts by describing the nature and prevalence of SYV within the case study cohort, before moving on to discuss the reasons for the high levels of SYV across the city. These include issues around territoriality and postcode rivalries, the role played by social media in the escalation of SYV and the importance that justice-involved young people place on gaining (and, crucially, on maintaining) status and reputation among their peers and within the wider community. The chapter also looks at the reasons why justice-involved young people might decide to carry a knife, before finishing with a discussion of the detrimental impact that carrying a knife has in terms of an increased likelihood of being a perpetrator and/or victim of SYV.

Chapter 5 starts by outlining the high prevalence of ACEs evident in the case study cohort. The most commonly identified ACEs are discussed, in particular the co-morbidity of some ACEs (such as, for example, physical abuse and witnessing domestic violence). The chapter also contains a discussion of the role of poverty and deprivation in SYV, before finishing with youth justice workers' views of the ACEs assessment tool.

Chapter 6 moves on to investigate the complex relationship between ACEs and SYV. It starts by looking at the psychological impact that ACEs can have. This includes feelings ranging from depression, shame and guilt, through to anger and aggression. The role of ACEs in the development of multiple diagnoses – including for example personality disorders, dissociation and psychosis – is also discussed. The chapter then moves on to look at the physiological impact of ACEs, including the relationship between ACEs and impaired neurodevelopment and the finding that justice-involved young people with ACEs frequently have a history of traumatic brain injury (TBI) alongside other neurodevelopmental disorders (NDDs). The detrimental impact of ACEs on the development and activation of the ventromedial prefrontal cortex and the hippocampus is discussed, along with the lasting damage that prolonged and consistent exposure to the 'fight-or-flight' hormones can cause to the developing brain. In addition to the impact that ACEs can have on a young person's mind and body, is the impact they can impact on a young person's identity formation. The problems that can result from inherent trauma – such as feelings of low self-worth and an over-reliance on praise and/ or acceptance from peers – is touched on before the chapter finishes with a discussion of the relevance and applicability of attachment theory to an investigation of ACEs and SYV.

Chapter 7, the final findings chapter, starts by discussing youth justice workers' understanding of the term 'trauma-informed practice' before outlining the strengths of a trauma-informed approach. The chapter then moves on to discuss the challenges and barriers to delivering trauma-informed practice with justice-involved young people. These include, for example, a young person refusing to talk about their ACEs, or being unable or unwilling to recognize any relationship between ACEs and their violent behaviour. Added to this is the sheer time it can take for a youth justice worker to build a sufficient trusted relationship with a young person that they might consider disclosing their ACEs, and how this process is constrained by short criminal justice sentences. The chapter then goes on to highlight the training and support needs of youth justice workers who are expected to work in a more trauma-informed way, in relation both to the skills needed to work more therapeutically, and the need for readily available clinical supervision for workers who may be struggling with vicarious trauma. The chapter finishes with a discussion of some of the wider barriers facing the implementation of trauma-informed practice within a youth justice context.

Chapter 8 brings together the preceding four chapters and concludes with policy and practice recommendations, before envisaging the future of trauma-informed practice in a youth justice context.

TWO

Review of the Literature

Serious youth violence

Youth violence and its impact on young people and communities remains a global challenge. The 2002 *World Report on Violence and Health* defines violence as the 'intentional use of physical force or power, threatened or actual, against another person or against a group or community, that either results in or has a high likelihood of resulting in injury, death, psychological harm, maldevelopment or deprivation' (Dahlberg and Krug 2002: 5). In the same report, youth violence is defined as 'violence that occurs among individuals aged 10–29 years who are unrelated and who may or may not know each other, and generally takes place outside of the home' (Mercy et al 2002: 25). Over two fifths of global homicides in 2020 affected those aged 10–29 years, with violence being the fourth leading cause of death in that age group (Salzburg Global Seminar 2022). However, deaths resulting from youth violence vary substantially at a global level. For example, across some countries of Latin America, the Caribbean and sub-Saharan Africa, estimates suggest that youth homicide rates are more than a hundred times higher than rates for countries in western Europe and the western Pacific (World Health Organization 2015: 6).

When it comes to the causes of serious youth violence (SYV), a meta-analysis by Hawkins et al (2000) identified a diverse range of factors that have been shown to increase the likelihood of a young person becoming involved in violence, either as a perpetrator or a victim. These factors were grouped into five domains: individual, family, school, peer-related, and community and neighbourhood factors. The *individual factors* included hyperactivity, concentration problems, restlessness and risk taking; aggressiveness; early initiation of violent behaviour; involvement in other forms of antisocial behaviour; and beliefs and attitudes favourable to deviant or antisocial behaviour. *Family factors* included separation from a parent, parental criminality, poor family management practices and low levels of parental involvement (Hawkins et al 2000). Indeed, hostile, harsh or rejecting parenting styles have been shown to increase the likelihood that a young person will become involved in SYV (Sitnick et al 2017). Being exposed to domestic violence, either as a victim or a witness, has also been found to increase the likelihood of a young person becoming involved in SYV (Weaver et al 2008).

The *school factors* identified by Hawkins et al (2000) included academic failure, truancy and dropping out of school. More recent research has also highlighted that disengagement and exclusion from education is related to an increased likelihood of a young person perpetrating or suffering SYV (Joliffe et al 2016; Irwin-Rogers and Harding 2018). When it comes to *peer-related factors*, Hawkins et al (2000) identified delinquent siblings, delinquent peers and gang membership, while their *community* and *neighbourhood factors* included poverty and community disorganization. Poverty has been shown to lead to feelings of rejection (by society), which can elicit shame and humiliation, both of which have been identified as fundamental and significant drivers of violence (Thomas 1995; Gilligan 2003). Additionally, an increasing lack of secure employment (Hudson-Sharp and Runge 2017) can lead to young people seeking out illegitimate ways to make money, such as through drug dealing and robbery (Irwin-Rogers et al 2020). Before moving on to look at SYV in England and Wales, it is important to be aware that the likelihood of a young person becoming involved in violence increases as the number of risk factors they exhibit or are exposed to increases (Farrington 1997). Added to this is the recent growth of smart-phone accessibility among young people and the concomitant rise in the use of social media, which has been shown to play a role in catalysing and triggering incidents of serious violence between young people (Irwin-Rogers and Pinkney 2017; Irwin-Rogers et al 2018).

As already touched on in the Introduction, in the context of England and Wales, findings from the Crime Survey for England and Wales (CSEW) show that levels of interpersonal violence have been declining since the mid-1990s (Billingham and Irwin-Rogers 2022). Yet, while interpersonal violence rates have fallen, SYV remains a growing concern in England and Wales. This concern is largely a result of knife and offensive weapon offences involving those aged 10–17 years rising year on year, from 2,639 in 2013 to 4,562 in 2019 (Ministry of Justice 2020). In the year ending September 2020, 248 people were stabbed to death in England and Wales (Home Office 2022). This increase has resulted in a sharp rise in the economic and social cost of SYV. In England and Wales, it was estimated that SYV generated a total economic and social cost of £1.3 billion in 2018/19; a rise of over 50 per cent since 2014/15 (Irwin-Rogers et al 2020).

Political and populist concerns about SYV in England and Wales have prompted the development of a raft of initiatives to tackle the problem. For example, in 2016 the cross-party Youth Violence Commission was established (Irwin-Rogers et al 2020), and in 2018 the cross-party Serious Violence Taskforce produced a *Serious Violence Strategy* (Home Office 2018). In 2019, the then prime minister Theresa May held an emergency 'Serious Violence Summit', before introducing dedicated Violence Reduction Units in areas worst affected by violent crime (Home Office 2020). Vast sums of government monies have been allocated to address SYV, such as an initial £35 million for Violence Reduction Units and £200 million to the Youth Endowment Fund.[1] In addition to this, at a legislative level Knife Crime Prevention Orders and Serious Violence Reduction Orders have also been introduced (Home Office 2022).[2]

Despite these responses to SYV, an enduring criticism has been the apparent lack of a coherent strategy that connects the various responses (for a fuller discussion see Dempsey 2021). This lack of coherence is troubling. SYV raises a multitude of issues concerning the stigmatizing of young people, societal attitudes, sensationalist media reporting and regional, national and global responses. The ways in which SYV is discussed, and more importantly understood, are critical to the responses to prevent and address it. As Billingham and Irwin-Rogers (2022: 6) note, 'discussions around "youth violence" can mobilise the term in a way which demonises, stigmatises, pathologises, patronises, or stereotypes young people, or in a way which generates profound misconceptions of violence, young people, and harm'. For instance, as noted in Chapter 1, for all the political and populist concerns about SYV over the last decade, it is only in the last few years that adverse childhood experiences (ACEs) have become part of the 'mainstream conversation' about SYV (Irwin-Rogers et al 2020: 76). With this in mind, this chapter will now go on to discuss the prevalence of ACEs among justice-involved young people, and the detrimental impact they can have.

Adverse childhood experiences

According to the Centers for Disease Control and Prevention (Centers for Disease Control and Prevention, n.d.), ACEs commonly refer to ten specific abuse, neglect and household dysfunctions to which someone is exposed prior to age 18, including: experiencing physical, emotional or sexual abuse; experiencing physical or emotional neglect; witnessing domestic violence; substance misuse within the family; mental health problems within the family; parental separation or loss; and having a family member in prison. The CDC-Kaiser Permanente Adverse Childhood Experiences (ACE) Study originated in southern California in the late 1990s. To this day, this study remains one of the largest investigations of childhood abuse and neglect and household challenges, and later-life health and well-being. The original study (Felitti et al 1998) used a ten-point scale to investigate the prevalence of three main categories of ACEs (see Figure 2.1). Each exposure is captured as a binary yes/no experience and combined into an ACE score that can range from 0 (no exposure to any of the ten ACEs) to 10 (exposure to all ten ACEs).

When it comes to the prevalence of ACEs, a study by the Early Intervention Foundation (Asmussen et al 2020) found that more than four fifths of the 399,500 young people who were identified as being in need in England in 2019 had experienced at least one ACE, with 54 per cent having experienced abuse or neglect. In terms of young people in the justice system, a Her Majesty's Inspectorate of Probation (2017: 8) inspection of Youth Offending Teams found that,[3] out of a sample of 115 young people who had committed violent, sexual and/or other offences where there were potential public protection issues, 81 per cent had experienced 'emotional trauma or other deeply distressing or disturbing things in their lives'. For example, one third had grown up in a household where there was a formal record of domestic abuse, and other traumatic experiences identified in the sample included separation and estrangement from parents, the death of a parent or main carer, sexual abuse, severe physical chastisement and parental substance misuse. If we look at those young people in the secure estate,[4] the prevalence of ACEs increases. For example, Martin et al (2021) explored the prevalence of ACEs within a sample of 58 young people admitted to a secure children's home in the north of England.[5] They found that, when compared to the general population, the young people were 1.85 times more likely to have experienced at least one ACE, and 13.08 times more likely to have experienced four or more ACEs. The same study also found that nearly all of the young people (97 per cent) had experienced at least one ACE and just over four fifths had experienced four or more, with the average ACE score being 5.55. The most common ACEs experienced by the sample

Figure 2.1: Types of ACEs

ABUSE | NEGLECT | HOUSEHOLD CHALLENGES

Physical

Emotional

Sexual

Physical

Emotional

Divorce

Mental illness

Parent treated violently

Incarcerated relative

Substance abuse

Source: Centers for Disease Control and Prevention, 2021

were parental separation (78 per cent), physical neglect (76 per cent), emotional abuse (71 per cent) and emotional neglect (69 per cent). A Prison Reform Trust study of 200 young people in custody (Jacobson et al 2010) found that just under two fifths had been on the child protection register and/or experienced abuse or neglect,[6] and 28 per cent had witnessed domestic violence. A study of 200 young people serving custodial sentences for Section 53 offences (Boswell 1996) found that just under three quarters of the sample had experienced some form of abuse or neglect,[7] and 57 per cent had experienced significant parental loss of contact or bereavement. Indeed, just over a third had experienced the 'double childhood trauma' of abuse/neglect and loss (Boswell 1996: 91). It is also important to note that ACEs occur in clusters and do so in predictable ways. For example, if a child is experiencing physical abuse, they are at far greater risk of experiencing emotional abuse and of witnessing domestic violence (Asmussen et al 2020).

ACEs have been shown to have lasting, negative effects on health and well-being. When it comes to mental health, Fox et al (2015) found that, while single ACEs did not necessarily increase the risk of developing mental health problems, the accumulation of multiple, different forms of ACE was responsible for the association between ACEs and mental health problems in justice-involved young people. Furthermore, research has found that each additional type of ACE exponentially increases the risk of developing mental health problems (Fox et al 2015; Perez et al 2018; Turner et al 2021). This has been found to be true for both internalized mental health problems, such as anxiety and depression, and externalized mental health problems, such as intermittent explosive disorder (defined as the pathological expression of reactive and impulsive aggression) (Turner et al 2021).

ACEs have also been found to be associated with offending behaviour. A study using data from the Cambridge Study in Delinquent Development found that those with at least one ACE were significantly more likely to have a higher number of total convictions than those without any ACEs and, as ACE scores increased, the mean number of life-course convictions also tended to increase (Craig et al 2017a). Moreover, ACEs have been shown to have an impact on the likelihood of future violence perpetration (Fox et al 2015), with each additional ACE increasing the risk of perpetrating violence by between 38 per cent (bullying) and 88 per cent (self-directed violence) for girls, and between 35 per cent (bullying) and 144 per cent (dating violence) for boys (Duke et al 2010). Indeed, it has been found that a higher ACE score significantly increases the odds of a child being classified as a serious violent offender (Perez et al 2018). In terms of which types of ACEs are most strongly associated with adolescent violence, Braga et al (2017) found that physical and sexual abuse was most strongly associated with violent and aggressive offending behaviours, while Maas et al (2008) found that compounded types of abuse (for example, physical, emotional and sexual) and greater severity of abuse increased the likelihood of later perpetrating youth violence.

When it comes to victims of youth violence, Baglivio et al (2021) found that young people who had suffered a greater number of ACEs were more likely to have committed a violent offence against multiple victim groups (in this instance, the groups included strangers, acquaintances/friends, romantic partner/ex-partner, family and authority figures) as opposed to a single victim group. In addition to this, each additional ACE has also been found to significantly increase the likelihood of self-directed violence (from 83 to 88 per cent for girls, and from 75 to 106 per cent for boys) (Duke et al 2010).[8] Other negative effects of ACEs that are relevant to this piece of research include the finding that cumulative trauma, as measured by an ACE score, represents a significant risk factor when it comes to gang involvement (Wolff et al 2020). Relatedly, higher ACE scores have also been found to be directly predictive of a child's level of admiration and imitation of deviant peers (Perez et al 2018). Interestingly, drawing on social control theory, Craig et al (2017b) investigated whether the relationship between ACEs and future offending could be moderated by protective factors resulting from social bonds. They found that those who are strongly bonded are more protected if they have less than five ACEs. However, if a strongly bonded child has more than five ACEs, then the protective effect is not strong enough to counteract the negative effects of ACEs outlined above.

Before moving on to look at trauma-informed practice, it is important to consider the relationship between ACEs, neurodiversity and violent offending behaviour. It has been found that ACEs can increase the chances of a child having three or more neurodivergent conditions (Kirby 2021). Indeed, emerging research has documented a relationship between exposure to childhood adversity and impaired neurodevelopment (SAMHSA 2014), with young people with ACEs having more neurodevelopmental disorders (NDDs) than those with no ACEs (Dinkler et al 2017). The word neurodivergence is an umbrella term that refers to the group of conditions that fall under the broader category of NDDs and includes, for example, attention deficit hyperactivity disorder (ADHD), autism spectrum disorder (ASD) and cognitive impairments attributable to traumatic brain injury (TBI). A Criminal Justice Joint Inspection review (2021: 8) noted that 'perhaps half of those entering prison could reasonably be expected to have some form of neurodivergent condition'. Rates among justice-involved young people are estimated to be higher, especially for ADHD and speech and language difficulties (Kirby 2021). This is important because ADHD has been found to be associated with violent offending (Cleaton and Kirby 2018), and young people with ADHD are less likely to appreciate the seriousness of their actions. Young people with ASD have also been found to be at increased risk of 'child criminal exploitation' (CCE) (see Chapter 6) (Kirby et al 2020).

The literature also shows that justice-involved young people with a history of ACEs frequently have a history of TBI alongside other NDDs (Kirby et al 2020). Indeed, ACEs are notably more common in those with a history of TBI than in those without (Williams et al 2018). It is estimated that around half the prison population have suffered a TBI, with domestic violence a leading cause among women (Criminal Justice Joint Inspection 2021). Among incarcerated young people, a systematic review found that the rates of TBI ranged from 17 per cent in an US study through to 72 per cent in an UK study (Hughes et al 2015b).[9] TBI also appears to be linked to greater risk of violent victimization. For example, Williams et al (2018) studied 197 incarcerated young people and found that three fifths reported a historic head injury, nearly half reported a historic loss of consciousness and just under a fifth reported moderate or severe TBI. The main cause of injury was violence. Vaughn et al (2014) similarly found that those justice-involved young people with TBI histories had more previous violent victimization experiences than those without. It is important to bear in mind the high prevalence of TBI among justice-involved young people because TBI has been found to be associated with higher impulsivity (Vaughn et al 2014), impulsive aggression, poor decision-making and lack of control of social behaviour (Williams et al 2018).

Trauma-informed practice

How a child is physically and/or psychologically affected by an ACE will contribute to whether it is experienced as traumatic. As defined by Substance Abuse and Mental Health Services Administration (SAMHSA) (2014: 7), trauma can result from 'an event, series of events, or set of circumstances that is experienced by an individual as physically or emotionally harmful or life threatening and that has lasting adverse effects on the individual's functioning and mental, physical, social, emotional, or spiritual well-being'. It is important to remember that any adverse effects might occur immediately or have a delayed onset, and they may be short- or long-term (SAMHSA 2014). Because of this, there has been a growing awareness in recent years of the importance of being trauma-informed when it comes to dealing with young people who have a history of ACEs. This is especially important for agencies who work with justice-involved young people (Liddle et al 2016; Cordis Bright 2017; Glendinning et al 2021).

The primary aim of a trauma-informed approach is to increase practitioners' awareness of how trauma might negatively impact a young person, and to reduce practices that might inadvertently retraumatize that child (Asmussen et al 2020). From a trauma-informed viewpoint, a child's behaviour needs to be understood in the context of coping strategies designed to survive adversity and overwhelming circumstances, whether these occurred in the past or are occurring currently (SAMHSA 2014). In essence, a trauma-informed approach necessitates a change of perspective from 'what's wrong with you?' to 'what happened to you?' (McCartan 2020). As one of the practitioner's guides from the Beyond Youth Custody programme succinctly summarizes (Wright et al 2016: 2):

> Trauma-informed practice may involve awareness raising and training, the provision of safe environments, reducing the scope for re-traumatisation and the coordination of provision designed to increase resilience and support. Trauma-informed approaches can be thought of as incorporating three key elements: an understanding of the prevalence of trauma; recognition of the effects of trauma both on those affected and on those who work with them; ... and the design of services which are informed by this knowledge.

Youth participation

Alongside the current focus on SYV, ACEs and trauma-informed practice is the growing call for the participation of justice-involved young people in the development of youth justice policy and practice. In England and Wales there has been a noticeable shift over the last decade in how young people in the justice system are viewed. Central to this shift is

Haines and Case's 'Child First, Offender Second' philosophy (2015: 45), founded on the belief that 'children are part of the solution, not part of the problem'. This philosophy is evident in the Youth Justice Board's (2020: 9) *Business Plan 2020/21*, which states that the 'experiences of children and the voice they bring is paramount to all that we do'. Similarly, the *Standards for Children in the Youth Justice System* (Ministry of Justice and Youth Justice Board 2019: 6) make it clear that youth justice agencies need to make sure that they 'encourage children's active participation'.

Research has shown that when participation, engagement and inclusion processes are co-created between young people and practitioners, efficacy can be achieved (Case and Haines 2015). Nevertheless, unlike in contexts such as health care that have a more established track-record of service user co-production and participation (Beckett et al 2018) young people in justice contexts are rarely given the opportunity to shape policy and service provision. An occasion where justice-involved young people were given the opportunity to influence youth justice practice resulted in the co-production of a framework of principles termed 'Participatory Youth Practice' (PYP) (Smithson et al 2021; Smithson and Jones 2021). PYP is predicated on six key principles: let them (young people) participate (in decision-making); always unpick why (their offending behaviour); acknowledge their limited life chances; help them to problem solve; help them to find better options; and develop their ambitions. By enabling justice-involved young people to participate meaningfully in decision-making processes, the PYP framework represents a formative step in the process of creating a justice system that respects and acknowledges young people. The PYP framework is now embedded in youth justice practice in England and Wales, and the six PYP principles underpinned the methodology that was adopted in this research.

THREE

Researching Adverse Childhood Experiences and Trauma

Research objectives

This research brings together the four areas outlined in Chapter 2 – serious youth violence (SYV), adverse childhood experiences (ACEs), trauma-informed practice and youth participation – to investigate the complex relationship between ACEs and SYV. Working in close collaboration with justice-involved young people and youth justice workers in Manchester, the research aimed to meet the following five objectives:

- To gauge the nature and prevalence of ACEs among justice-involved young people in Manchester.
- To explore young people's own articulations of the causes and drivers of SYV.
- To develop a deeper understanding of the relationship between ACEs and SYV.
- To explore young people's experiences of current youth justice practice, in particular their experiences of trauma-informed practice.
- To co-create with justice-involved young people a resource for youth justice workers.

To meet these five research objectives, a mixed-methods approach was adopted that incorporated quantitative, qualitative and participatory elements. The quantitative element of the research focussed on data collected using a bespoke ACEs assessment tool that was developed specifically for the project.

The qualitative element had two strands: semi-structured interviews with youth justice workers and narrative interviews with justice-involved young people. The participatory element of the research was a series of creative workshops involving justice-involved young people, the research team, drama therapists and a professional sports coach.

The fieldwork for the research was conducted over a 15-month period between January 2020 and March 2021. The research was originally a 12-month study (scheduled for completion in December 2020) but, owing to the COVID-19 pandemic and the subsequent restrictions, a three-month extension was agreed to enable the research team to undertake the necessary fieldwork and data collection. Ethical approval for the research was granted by Manchester Metropolitan University's research ethics and governance committee.

The ACEs assessment tool

To enable the research to meet the first research objective it was necessary to devise a way to assess the nature and prevalence of ACEs among justice-involved young people in Manchester. Much of the evidence linking ACEs with negative outcomes comes from studies that measure adults' recollections of childhood adversity. While the validity of such retrospective measures has been questioned, because adults are often poor at recalling experiences of ACEs (Asmussen et al 2020), prospective measures have been shown to overcome this issue (Reuben et al 2016). With this in mind, a bespoke ACEs assessment tool was developed in partnership with youth justice workers at Manchester Youth Justice. The tool itself (see Figure 3.1) was based on the ten-point scale used in the original Adverse Childhood Experiences (ACE) Study from the late 1990s (Felitti et al 1998) – each of the ACEs from the original study was included in the assessment tool – but, in addition to the simple, binary yes/no to each ACE that characterized the original study, the assessment tool

Figure 3.1: The ACEs assessment tool©

ACEs Trauma Portfolio			Total Number of ACEs =
Case ID	**Chronology**		**Offence Details**
CV ID Number: Age: Court Order: Team Locality: Gender: Ethnicity:	Date of Screening:		

ACEs Intelligence Portfolio

ACEs Trauma Portfolio		ACEs Intelligence Portfolio	
Emotional Abuse Yes ☐ No ☐	Source of Information: Description:	**Mental Illness within the Family** Yes ☐ No ☐	Source of Information: Description:
Physical Abuse Yes ☐ No ☐	Source of Information: Description:	**Family Member in / been in Prison** Yes ☐ No ☐	Source of Information: Description:
Sexual Abuse Yes ☐ No ☐	Source of Information: Description:	**Parental Separation / Loss** Yes ☐ No ☐	Source of Information: Description:
Emotional Neglect Yes ☐ No ☐	Source of Information: Description:	**Substance Use by Family** Yes ☐ No ☐	Source of Information: Description:
Physical Neglect Yes ☐ No ☐	Source of Information: Description:	**Witnessed Domestic Violence** Yes ☐ No ☐	Source of Information: Description:

Further Notable Information	Prevalence	Source of Information	Description

also captures offence details, the source of the information and a description for each of the ten ACEs. Between 11 January 2020 and 10 January 2021, a total of 200 young people were assessed using the tool. At the end of the 12-month data collection period, the data collected by the tool was exported to IBM-SPSS Statistics for analysis.[1]

It is important to note that the ACEs assessment tool was completed by youth justice workers on behalf of the young people on their caseload, rather than by the young people themselves. This is because research has found that young people with a history of ACEs report more frequent feelings of upset when completing personal survey questions about their childhood than those without these experiences (Langhinrichsen-Rohling et al 2006). Furthermore, it has been found that, as the number of ACEs increases, so do the levels of distress and discomfort. For example, Skar et al (2019) investigated levels of upset following routine ACE screening using the Child and Adolescent Trauma Screen questionnaire in Norwegian youth mental health clinics. They found that those young people who had been exposed to any type of ACE reported levels of upset significantly higher than those reported by subjects who had no ACEs, with a higher number of ACEs associated with a higher level of upset. Likewise, a study in the USA by Mersky et al (2019) found that young people with a history of ACEs were more likely to report discomfort when completing an ACE questionnaire than those without. Their analysis similarly found that each additional reported ACE was associated with significantly greater discomfort. Bearing in mind the high prevalence of ACEs identified in studies of justice-involved young people in both the USA (Duke et al 2010; Dierkhising et al 2013; Baglivio et al 2014; Fox et al, 2015) and the UK (Boswell 1996; Jacobson et al 2010; Her Majesty's Inspectorate of Probation 2017; Martin et al 2021), it was felt that asking young people to complete the assessment themselves could be potentially upsetting and might cause them distress and discomfort.

To further reduce the risk of upsetting the young people that were being assessed, the ACEs assessment was not undertaken by a young person's youth justice worker in dialogue with the young person. Instead, the workers used the information that they routinely collect for AssetPlus to complete the ACEs tool. AssetPlus is an integrated assessment and planning framework that was developed by the Youth Justice Board in 2014 (Baker 2012; Youth Justice Board 2014) to assist youth justice workers in assessing and planning for the young people in their care. Using information that is routinely collected to complete the ACEs assessment tool meant that the young people did not need to be explicitly asked about their ACEs and the workers did not need the young people to be present to complete the tool.

Importantly, the ACEs tool was also a 'live' document that could be updated as and when a youth justice worker found out more information about a young person. This was a particularly important feature as it allowed for a more accurate assessment of ACEs. As will be discussed in Chapter 7, it can often take a significant period of time for a young person with ACEs to build a sufficient trusted relationship with their youth justice worker to start to disclose ACEs. As such, it was essential that the ACEs tool was not simply completed once, at the initial assessment point, before the young person had been given the time to build a relationship with their worker.

The ACEs assessment tool was only completed for those young people whose cases with the Manchester Youth Justice Service were 'open' between 11 January 2020 and 10 January 2021. This meant all new cases that started between these two dates, as well as all cases that had started before 11 January 2020 but finished between the two dates. Data provided by the Manchester Youth Justice Service showed a total of 424 cases open between the opening and closing dates of the study, indicating that the ACEs assessment tool was completed for just under half (47 per cent) of all the cases available for analysis.

Table 3.1: Comparison of all open cases and ACEs assessment cases

		All open cases (n=424)	ACEs assessment cases (n=200)
Age	Under 15	18%	10%
	15	19%	14%
	16	28%	27%
	17	31%	35%
	18	4%	14%
Gender	Male	90%	90%
	Female	10%	10%
Ethnicity	White	55%	54%
	Black	19%	22%
	Mixed	15%	16%
	Asian	7%	6%
	Other	4%	2%
SYV offence	Yes	44%	49%
	No	56%	51%

To check that those young people for whom an ACEs assessment was completed were representative of all open cases during the data collection period, a comparison was made between all the open cases and the ACEs assessment cases. As can be seen (see Table 3.1), the sample of young people for whom an ACEs assessment was carried out were broadly representative (in terms of age, gender, ethnicity and having committed a SYV offence) of all the cases that were open to the Manchester Youth Justice Service between 11 January 2020 and 10 January 2021. This was particularly important in relation to the proportion of young people who had committed a SYV offence, as this research did not want to over-represent the prevalence of ACEs and SYV in the Manchester youth justice cohort.

The qualitative interviews

As already mentioned, the qualitative element of the research involved semi-structured interviews with youth justice workers and narrative interviews with justice-involved young people. While the aim of the interviews with the workers was to explore their views on the relationship between ACEs and SYV, the narrative interviews aimed to explore young people's own articulations of the causes and drivers of SYV and their experiences of trauma-informed practice within the youth justice system. The narrative interviews also aimed to explore the young people's views on how ACEs and SYV might be related.

Interviews with youth justice workers

Semi-structured interviews were undertaken with a range of youth justice workers. Owing to the COVID-19 restrictions, all of the interviews were undertaken remotely using MS Teams rather than face-to-face as originally planned. During June and July 2020, ten interviews were undertaken with youth justice workers. In addition, interviews were undertaken with two drama therapists from the emotional trauma support team at One Education.[2] As will be discussed in Chapter 7, at the time of the research these therapists were commissioned by the Manchester Youth Justice Service to deliver clinical interventions to justice-involved young people in Manchester. In total, 12 interviews were undertaken. These ranged in length from 54 to 109 minutes. All the interviews were digitally recorded, fully transcribed and analysed in NVivo using template analysis (Brooks and King 2014).[3]

Narrative interviews with justice-involved young people

There is a growing body of research around life stories and narratives. The components of this work include life narratives, constructed by individuals to convey meaningful perceptions of self, identity and reality, making it likely that concepts of identity are embedded within narrative discourse (Chase 2005). Narrative identity is the story of the self that weaves together the reconstructed past, the perceived present and the imagined future, providing an individual with a sense of unity and meaning (McAdams 1995).

Narratives are not simply converging measures of identity; narratives are constitutive of identity, in that how we make sense of our experiences and who we perceive ourselves to be are reciprocally related across development (McAdams and Pals 2006). Life narratives are unique because they show the relationship between life events and the development of the storyteller's personality, including how the individual makes life decisions according to central values (Habermas and Silveira 2008). A person's internalized and evolving life story integrates the reconstructed past and imagined future to provide life with some degree of unity and purpose (McAdams and McLean 2013). The McAdams Life Story Interview (Bauer and McAdams 2004) is a methodological concept which helps us to understand narrative identity. It is a tool that has been widely used in psychological research that emphasizes narrative and the storied nature of human conduct. Narratives allow researchers to ethically and meaningfully understand lived experiences in context (Fivush and Merrill 2016). Because of this, the McAdams approach was particularly suited to this research with its focus on ACEs and their relationship to SYV. Furthermore, it was felt that the McAdams approach would better enable the research to meet the research objectives than a more traditional semi-structured interview.

The research team are very experienced in delivering narrative interviews with justice-involved young people (Gray 2008; Jump 2014). However, owing to COVID-19 restrictions, it was not possible to undertake these interviews as originally planned. To ensure that justice-involved young people could still be interviewed it was decided that the team should train youth justice workers to deliver the interviews on our behalf. The training was promoted to workers and 14 signed up. The general feeling was that learning these interviewing skills would help their personal development and potentially improve their practice. In July 2020, a two-hour training session on narrative interviewing was delivered via MS Teams to the 14 volunteers. To give the workers the skills and confidence to deliver the interviews on our behalf, the training included the underlying theory behind the McAdams Life Story Interview method, how to deliver the method in practice, a Q-and-A around the interview guide and a discussion around ethics and informed consent. Ongoing post-training support was offered to all of the workers.

Between July 2020 and January 2021 a total of nine narrative interviews were carried out by youth justice workers (see Table 3.2). Despite the workers engaging with many young people during this period, a large proportion of the young people did not want to be interviewed, did not want to have their interview recorded and/or did not want to partake in the interview remotely. This final issue was exacerbated by the COVID-19 restrictions that limited the amount and type of face-to-face contact that workers could have with the young people on their caseload. As a result of these factors, many young people did not consent to be interviewed. The nine interviews that were undertaken were all transcribed and analysed thematically in NVivo using template analysis (Brooks and King 2014).

The participatory workshops

To centre the voices of justice-involved young people in this research, it was essential that a participatory approach was adopted. As will be described in detail below, a series of creative workshops were designed and delivered to two separate groups of young people.

Table 3.2: Narrative interview participants

ID	Age	Gender	Ethnicity	Offence	ACEs
CH1	17	Male	White	Section 18 assault[4]	9
CH2	17	Male	White	Robbery	6
CH3	17	Male	Mixed	Robbery and Section 18 assault	6
CH4	17	Male	Black	Robbery and possession of a firearm	6
CH5	17	Male	White	Section 18 assault and attempted kidnapping	5
CH6	15	Male	Mixed	Attempted Section 18 assault	8
CH7	15	Male	White	Possession of a knife and public order	N/K[5]
CH8	17	Male	Black	Violent disorder	0
CH9	17	Male	White	Possession of a knife	6

Designing the workshops

The research team have considerable experience of using participatory research methods to work with young people in the youth justice system. Our work across the Greater Manchester region has led to transformative action in practice (Vaughan 2014), demonstrated through the co-creation with justice-involved young people of the Participatory Youth Practice (PYP) framework (see Chapter 2). Underpinned by the PYP principles, the research team set about organizing the participatory workshops. Between November 2020 and March 2021 four workshops were delivered. Owing to COVID-19 restrictions, the first and second workshops were held at Manchester Metropolitan University's Platt Lane Sports Complex. These facilities were COVID-secure and, as will be discussed below, enabled us to incorporate sport-based activities into the workshops. The third and fourth workshops were conducted online via MS Teams.

With our youth justice colleagues, the team identified and subsequently invited young people who, at the time of the project, were engaged with the Manchester Youth Justice Service for SYV offences. Using the participatory principle of the adult facilitator acting in a 'support role' (Ozer 2016: 264), the team identified professional facilitators for these workshops. Working very closely with three drama therapists from One Education (two of whom have been commissioned by Manchester Youth Justice – see Chapter 7) and a professional sports coach from Manchester Metropolitan University, the research team designed and delivered the first two participatory workshops. This is the first time in the UK that drama therapy and sport have been used together with justice-involved young people.

When working with young people in therapeutic settings, expressive techniques such as play, music, storytelling and art therapies are often used (Mendoza and Bradley 2021). The drama therapy element adopted in the first and second workshops was storytelling. The drama therapists often use storytelling as a technique in their work and, given the sensitive nature of the research – that is, ACEs and SYV – the decision was made to use the 6-Part Story Method (6PSM) (Dent-Brown and Wang 2006). This approach involves a patient, in a therapeutic setting, creating a story that is used to elicit further discussion (Gersie 1992). Storytelling is viewed as an effective approach to concentrate on fictional, third-person accounts and provide metaphors rather than a description of actual lived events (Dwivedi 1997). This was felt to be a particularly appropriate method for discussing the issue of ACEs and being a perpetrator and/or victim of SYV. As one of the drama therapists noted, "The six-part story method creates distance between the young person and the material being explored and therefore provides safety to work with trauma and painful narratives." The six elements of the method (Dent-Brown and Wang 2006) involve creating:

1. a main character in some setting;
2. a task for the main character;
3. obstacles in the main character's way;
4. things that help the main character;
5. the climax or main action of the story; and
6. the consequences or aftermath of the story.

Based on our previous research experience, the team decided that in addition to the storytelling, sporting activities should be incorporated into the workshops to engage the young people. Within a contemporary UK context, it is well documented that sport in general is useful as a tool for engaging young people, in particular boys already involved in, or at risk of involvement in, criminality and violence (Meek 2018; Jump 2020). The research team had already used sport in several previous research projects working with justice-involved young people (Jump and Smithson 2020; Smithson et al 2021). At the time of undertaking this research, the team were involved in a large project, funded by Comic Relief, that utilized rugby as a means of engaging with justice-involved young people across Greater Manchester.[6] Given the success of the rugby project, and the ability of the professional sports coach on the project to effectively engage with justice-involved young people, the team invited him to take part in designing and delivering the workshops for this research. To further engage the young people, each person who attended the workshops received three qualifications via AQA's Unit Award Scheme.[7] These were for 'group work', 'basic rugby skills' and 'strength and conditioning'.

Workshop participants

Prior to the workshops, the research team provided promotional materials to the youth justice workers so that they could gauge the interest of the young people they work with. Eight young people showed an interest in the first workshop and were signed up by their youth justice worker to attend, and a further eight young people were signed up to attend the second workshop. However, on the day, only five attended the first workshop (see Table 3.3) and only two attended the second one (see Table 3.4). This was despite the research team arranging taxis to pick the young people up from their home address and take them to and from the workshops, incentives being offered (in the form of high street vouchers and the opportunity to earn three AQA qualifications) and food and drink being provided. While disappointing, lower-than-promised levels of attendance are to be expected when undertaking participatory research with justice-involved young people whose often chaotic lives can impact upon their ability and/or willingness to engage, something that the research team had experienced when

Table 3.3: Workshop 1 participants

ID	Age	Gender	Ethnicity	Offence	ACEs
Participant 1	18	Male	White	Section 18 grievous bodily harm (GBH)	9
Participant 2	16	Male	White	Robbery	6
Participant 3	17	Male	Mixed	Possession of a knife	5
Participant 4	16	Male	Black	Robbery and possession of a knife	6
Participant 5	16	Male	White	Section 18 GBH and false imprisonment	5

Table 3.4: Workshop 2 participants

ID	Age	Gender	Ethnicity	Offence	ACEs
Participant 1	14	Male	White	Assault	3
Participant 2	18	Male	Mixed	Robbery	6

undertaking the co-creation of the PYP framework (Jump and Smithson 2020; Smithson et al 2021).

Delivering the workshops

The first and second workshops (undertaken in November and December 2020) commenced with some very informal sporting activities run by the sports coach. This was followed by a discussion about who everyone was, the aims of the research and the purpose of the workshop. After introductions, everyone embarked on some 'ice-breaker' activities and some more sporting activities. The group then sat in a horseshoe shape to begin the storytelling process. The drama therapists explained the storytelling approach and how they would support the young people in producing their story. In both workshops, the storytelling was divided into two one-hour sessions with a lunch break in the middle. The first session was to create the six-part story. Working through the six elements of the 6PSM described above, the young people were encouraged and supported to develop their story. Rather than follow a linear approach, they were presented with the ending of the story first: a young person had been the victim of a serious violent assault. Throughout the storytelling process, one of the drama therapists illustrated the various parts of the story. These illustrations were produced in parallel with the storytelling and it was observed that they provided a focal point when the young people did not want to make eye contact with either the research team or each other.

Following lunch, the second session was used to discuss the story with the young people. The story was used as a resource to elicit further discussion (Gersie 1992) about the young people's own experiences and views of SYV. This included, for example, discussions about why young people might become involved in SYV, the impact of perpetrating a SYV offence and their experiences of ACEs. After each of the two sessions, the young people were also actively encouraged to take part in the sporting activities run by the sports coach so that they could obtain their AQA qualifications. It was observed that taking part in the sporting activities provided the young people with a physical and emotional release from the sensitive material that constituted the six-part stories. The first and second workshops ended with a reflexive discussion with the young people about their involvement in the workshop and checking in with them to make sure that they had not been adversely affected by the workshops. It was emphasized to the young people that they could contact the drama therapists and/or their youth justice worker if they needed to speak to anyone about the issues and experiences that had been raised in the workshops.

The six-part stories

As outlined above, the 6PSM utilized in the first two workshops resulted in the creation of two fictional stories, one from each workshop. As the method dictated, the young people from each workshop fleshed out the ending of the story first. In the first workshop, the story ended with a young person named Jack being stabbed multiple times. In the second workshop, the ending saw a young person named Joe being kidnapped by a group of older young people. What follows is an overview of the two six-part stories that were created. 'Story 1: Jack and Paul' was developed in the first workshop (see Figure 3.2), 'Story 2: Joe's kidnap' in the second (see Figure 3.3).

Analysing the emergent themes from the first two workshops

Following the creation of the six-part stories in the first half of the workshops, the second half was used to discuss the stories with the young people, with the story being used as a tool to elicit further discussion about their own experiences and

Figure 3.2: Story 1 – Jack and Paul

Figure 3.3: Story 2 – Joe's kidnap

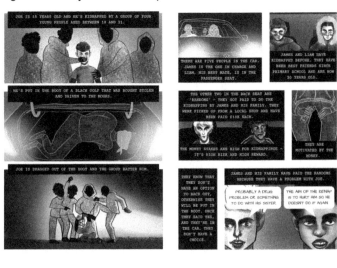

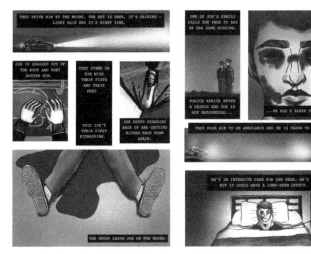

views of SYV. These discussions were digitally recorded and transcribed. Other documentation from the workshops in the form of flip-chart exercises and the illustrations produced by the drama therapist were also collated to assist with the analysis process. Owing to COVID-19 restrictions in December 2020 and the subsequent challenges of arranging to meet with the young people, the initial stage of data analysis was completed by the research team, rather than in partnership with the participants as originally planned (Foster-Fishman et al 2005). The materials from the two workshops were analysed thematically (Braun and Clarke 2006) and a set of emergent themes identified.

The second stage of the analysis took place approximately three months after the original two workshops. During this time, and with the support of our youth justice colleagues, the research team remained in touch with the young participants. They were all invited to partake in a third workshop to help analyse the findings from the first two workshops. Unfortunately, owing to COVID-19 restrictions, the third workshop had to be delivered remotely. Thanks to evolving circumstances in which some of them found themselves and/ or a reluctance to take part remotely, the majority of young people turned down the invitation to participate in this stage of the research. Only one participant from the first workshop agreed to be involved in the third.

Using MS Teams, the research team met with him and shared the emergent themes. It was heavily emphasized that these themes were just for consolidation, and open to challenge and change. Working together with the research team, he changed and challenged some of the themes, before ranking them in order of importance (see Tables 3.5 to 3.9).

Bearing in mind the positive outcomes associated with using methods such as Photovoice (Catalani and Minkler 2010), the research team wanted to use animation and narration to capture visually the young people's stories and their subsequent discussions. During the fourth and final workshop, the team

Table 3.5: The main reasons for young people's involvement in violence

1. Money

2. Wanting to be someone

3. There's no other way

4. Loyalty to heads and elders

5. Pressure

Table 3.6: During an act of violence young people are thinking

1. They are not thinking, they are reacting on impulse

2. Not thinking about the consequences until afterwards

3. Kill or be killed

4. Flight or fight

Table 3.7: What ACEs have young people who have been involved in violence had?

1. Witnessing domestic violence

2. Parental separation/loss

3. Familial substance use

Table 3.8: Types of support needed by young people

1. Trauma-based therapy

2. Understanding of the reasons why they committed the violence

3. Understanding of childhood experiences

worked with a professional to animate the two six-part stories that the young people had created. The end result is a ten-minute animation that youth justice workers can use

Table 3.9: Who needs to offer the support?

1. Someone whom a child has a relationship with

2. Youth justice workers

3. Schools

4. Police

when discussing ACEs and SYV with the young people on their caseload (see the fifth research objective at the start of this chapter).[8] A comic-book version of the animation is also available.[9]

FOUR

Serious Youth Violence

Level and type of serious youth violence

> There has always been some level of serious youth violence
> [in Manchester] but it certainly seems that there is more now.
> (Youth justice worker [YJW] 3)

As noted in Chapter 2, levels of violence in England and Wales have been declining since the mid-1990s (Billingham and Irwin-Rogers 2022). Yet, while violence rates have fallen, serious youth violence (SYV) remains a growing concern in England and Wales. As already mentioned, the Youth Justice Board define SYV as 'any drug, robbery or violence against the person offence that has a gravity score of five of more'. Levels of SYV have been rising in England and Wales, and figures show that both perpetrators and victims of these offences are getting younger, with self-reported violence peaking at age 15 (Home Office 2018).

In July 2019, the Youth Justice Board released data on all proven SYV offences for the 12 youth justice services that form the Serious Youth Violence Reference Group,[1] of which Manchester is one.[2] The data showed that the number of SYV offences in Manchester had risen by over 200 per cent between 2016/17 and 2018/19. Alongside this, the rate of SYV (per 10,000 10- to 17-year-olds in the general population) had risen dramatically in Manchester, with the city having the highest rate of SYV in 2018/19 within the Reference Group. Indeed, a fifth of all youth offences in Manchester in 2018/19 were SYV, with the most common being robbery, followed by violence and then drugs.

As outlined in Table 3.1, the adverse childhood experiences (ACEs) assessment tool showed that almost exactly half (n=99) of the 200 young people who were assessed between 11 January 2020 and 10 January 2021 had committed a SYV offence. The high proportion of SYV cases was also highlighted in the interviews with youth justice workers:

Interviewer [I]:   What percentage of your caseload right now are SYV?

YJW 9:   I think at least 40 per cent. I'm trying to work it out ... Yes, 40 or 50 per cent, like half.

In addition to the high levels of SYV, a number of workers commented on the fact that more first-time entrants (FTEs)[3] appeared to be coming into the youth justice system with SYV offences, as opposed to the more minor offences that had previously been associated with FTEs:

YJW 1:   Back in the day, the first-time offence would be something quite minor. These days, you're getting really, really young people ... coming through the system for the first time with really serious offences [like] kidnap.

I: Are you getting many first-time entrants with robberies?

YJW 9:   Yes, I can think of at least two on my caseload who are first-time robberies.

The observation that more FTEs appear to be coming into the youth justice system for SYV offences is reflected in the *Youth Justice Statistics 2020/21* (Youth Justice Board and Ministry of Justice 2022). According to the statistics, the offences committed by FTEs that have seen the largest percentage point increases over the last ten years are possession of a weapon, drug offences, violence against the person and robbery.

When it comes to the types of SYV offence that were committed in Manchester, of the 99 assessed young people who had committed a SYV offence, over two thirds (n=67) had committed a robbery, over a fifth (n=23) a violent offence, and just under a tenth (n=9) a drugs offence. This was reflected in the interviews with youth justice workers:

YJW 9:   I've got quite a few on my caseload ... for robberies with an offensive weapon, ... [and] Section 18 assaults.

I: What are some of the offences that young people are presenting with?

YJW 4:   Knives is probably the highest one at the moment. Dealing Class-A drugs is creeping up as well. Robbery is [also] high.

In relation to different areas of Manchester, one youth justice worker observed that while the south of the city appeared to be characterized by robberies, the more ethnically diverse areas in the centre appeared to be characterized by territorial violence. This is concerning as Manchester has a long history of using the term 'gang' to label groups of Black, Asian and minority ethnic (BAME) young people (Smithson et al 2013; Williams 2015). This has led to the over-policing of certain geographical areas, including the disproportionate use of stop and search tactics (Lammy Review 2017; Tiratelli et al 2018). Notwithstanding this worker's observation, the analysis of the data collected by the ACEs assessment tool revealed that neither ethnicity nor area of the city were associated with statistically significant differences in prevalence of SYV.[4]

Reasons for serious youth violence

The issue of territoriality was highlighted by a number of workers as a key reason for SYV in the city. These 'postcode rivalries' appeared to come to the fore when young people had to travel across the city:

YJW 4: There's a lot of the postcode rivalries ... The whole "where are you from?" is a massive factor in Manchester ... I do think that does influence the violence.

YJW 6: Young people quite openly talk to me about feeling cautious or worrying about travelling to certain parts of the city.

YJW 4: One of my young people was passing [through an area] on a bus. He knew he shouldn't have been going through that route, so he was sat on the top deck with his hood on, [but] three people from that area got on the bus and stabbed him. They said "You're in the wrong area. You shouldn't be here."

Despite these territorial rivalries having existed between some of these areas for many years, one of the workers felt that the current rise in social media use among young people was exacerbating existing rivalries through the facilitation of disagreements or "beef":

YJW 7: Territory and areas have always been there, ... [but] I just think things are exacerbated through social media. I feel that a lot of the beef is happening because people are chatting on social media, because they can say what they want, and then when they see that person [face-to-face], then we're seeing the violence.

The role of social media in SYV offences was highlighted in a Her Majesty's Inspectorate of Probation (2017: 9) thematic inspection that noted the 'strong influence social media has on young people who commit serious offences'. The inspection found that in one quarter of the cases that were examined the young person's use of social media was directly related to the offence they had committed, with social media identified as the catalyst for some of the most serious and violent offences. The inspection also identified how SYV often took place when young people met face-to-face on the street or on public transport following arguments or personal abuse that had taken place on social media. Indeed, there is evidence to suggest that rival groups use social media to promote and incite violence (Densley 2020).

Both the workers and young people that were interviewed for this research talked about social media being used to promote and publicize fights that had been filmed on smart-phones and then uploaded to YouTube, TikTok or Snapchat (Irwin-Rogers et al 2018):

YJW 3: I had a guy yesterday who was telling me "I had a fight in Tesco car park, it's on YouTube", and he showed it to me.

The filming of fights was also highlighted in the first participatory workshop. When discussing Paul, the lead character in the six-part story (see Figure 3.2), and his previous experiences of humiliating and filming victims, the young people stated the following:

Paul is aware that robberies can happen for a number of reasons. Sometimes it can be to humiliate another young person. He has been involved in these tasks and has stripped victims of their clothes and filmed them. He knows that the stripping is the humiliation, and the victim has to live with that every day, night and day. It will go everywhere. TikTok, Snapchat. There is no coming back from it. It's violation on the highest level.

As will be discussed in the following section, the ever-present possibility of having robberies and fights filmed and posted on social media often resulted in young people making the decision to carry a weapon (primarily a knife). While this was principally to protect themselves from being victimized in the first place, it was also to avoid the potential humiliation of being victimized, having it filmed and the film being seen "everywhere". Although the vast majority of social media usage among young people is unrelated to SYV, there are instances where social media is used for the purpose of humiliation and/or retaliation. This has been exacerbated by the growth of smart-phone accessibility among young people, which provides an unlimited opportunity for rivals to antagonize each other on a large scale and over a prolonged period (Frey 2018), thus leading to a cycle of victimization and retaliation (Irwin-Rogers and Pinkney 2017).

As evidenced in the participatory workshops, young people appeared to be fully aware of the harm that being victimized could potentially have on their reputation. As noted in the first workshop, if this occurs, "there is no coming back from it" for the victim:

I: Why do you think respect is so important to these young people?

YJW 5: It's about their own identity. Having a place. If you're disrespected, you don't have a place. Maintaining respect gives them a place within their group. It shows their ranking.

For those young people who are victimized, swift retaliation is imperative to avoid a loss of reputation. Indeed, if a young person is shamed through victimization, retaliation is primarily a reassertion of selfhood and pride (Gilligan 1997). As highlighted in the second quote below, being stabbed outside school appeared to make the victim angry rather than scared. It is likely that this was because he had been humiliated in front of his peers outside the school gates, and the negative impact this is likely to have had on his reputation:

YJW 3:	The young person who committed the stabbing [offence] had been a victim of stabbing himself a couple of months back.
I:	Where were you stabbed?
Young person [YP] 7:	It was outside of school ... They [some boys] were screaming stuff from across the road at me so I ended up approaching them and then they started to push me and circle me ...
I:	What happened next?
YP 7:	We were in a fight for a little bit and then one of them grabbed a knife out and stabbed me ...
I:	That sounds like a really scary experience ...
YP 7:	I was mostly just angry. I'm still pretty angry.

The topic of reputation elicited much discussion in the second participatory workshop. In line with research that highlights how violence is often employed to solidify an identity of toughness and a reputation for violence (Wilkinson 2001), the young people in the workshop spoke of those as young as 11 years of age "getting involved in shit to get a name" because "everybody wants a name for themselves". This point was also raised in the interviews with youth justice workers:

YJW 3:	Rather than financial gain, it [committing a robbery] is as much about gaining respect amongst your friends.

The young people in the second workshop also talked about how "some people don't give a shit – they just go out and do all sorts for a reputation". Interestingly, during the third workshop, the theme of "wanting to be someone" was ranked as the second most important reason why a young person might perpetrate a SYV offence (see Table 3.5). This was evidenced in the first workshop, when the young people were discussing Paul's initial decision to commit the robbery:

Paul has been tasked with robbing a random [stranger] by an older [person]. It is an opportunity for him to become someone and if he backs out, he will lose all credibility and his reputation. Paul keeps getting asked to do things by the heads and the olders, and he is keen to climb the ranks.

Reasons for carrying a knife

Bearing in mind the reasons for SYV outlined above, it becomes perhaps more understandable why a young person might decide to carry a knife. Indeed, the high prevalence of knife possession was identified in the data collected by the ACEs assessment tool. Out of the 200 young people who were assessed, three tenths (n=60) had been charged with 'possession of a knife/bladed article'. As highlighted below, for some young people, being armed with a knife made committing crime easier:

YJW 6:   One young man I work with said "a knife is a very good way of getting what I want without having to say anything". He would just show his knife and say, "give me your phone", and the phone would be handed over. So, for him, it was a very straightforward, quick way of getting what he wanted.

However, for the vast majority, their decision to carry a knife or other weapon/s appeared to be governed by fear of victimization and, as discussed earlier, humiliation and "violation on the highest level":

YJW 7: They're scared of being attacked. They're scared of being humiliated ... And the knock-on effect is ... young people are carrying knives and weapons, through fear of other young people carrying knives and weapons.

YJW 2: A recent case [of mine] was picked up [by the police] ... with an axe in his bag ... and a ten-inch knife as well ... What has come out of his case is [that] he doesn't feel safe going from one place to another.

The role of fear in a young person's decision to carry a knife was repeatedly highlighted by the youth justice workers. Nearly all of the workers interviewed reported young people on their caseload carrying knives because they were scared and wanted to be able to protect themselves. This is supported by recent research that found young people often start carrying knives to avoid becoming victims (Traynor 2016). Other research has found that young people view knife-carrying as a legitimate response to potential threats (Brennan and Moore 2009). In this instance, carrying a knife is viewed as harm prevention and being streetwise. Indeed, to *not* carry a knife is deemed irresponsible (Riggs and Palasinski 2011).

YJW 4: They're very casual about it ... They'll just say "if I don't carry a knife, I'm just not going to be safe. I'm putting myself in danger. Someone will pull a knife on me."

YJW 8: I had one young lad who said "everybody carries knives nowadays, and if you get into an argument, they'll just whip a knife out. So, I'd rather have one too."

YJW 5: I do get a lot of them carrying knives ... They say "everybody's doing it, ... so therefore I'm doing it. If I have a fight with somebody at least I'm tooled. At least I can defend myself."

This view that "everybody" is carrying a knife was supported by the young people in the second participatory workshop. In the second half of the workshop, the discussion organically turned to the subject of carrying knives, and the two participants gave their views on why young people carry them:

> I started carrying knives in Year 9. But now you see kids in Year 7, never been in trouble in their lives, carrying a knife because they see other people carrying them. They're thinking "if they're carrying one, then it must be important for me to carry one."
>
> People have different opinions on it. I know people who won't carry a knife at all, because they would rather fight with their fists, but then other people won't leave their house without a knife, out of fear and revenge.
>
> Or you might carry one because someone you know who has a beef with you is carrying one [and] you just want to use it on him, and that's just how it is.

It would appear that carrying a knife has become almost normalized among justice-involved young people. As noted by a number of the workers, it has become a habit for many young people:

YJW 10: Some of them just see it [carrying a knife] as a normal behaviour. Once you get into a routine, it's hard to break. If you're used to carrying a knife, you're not going to not carry a knife, are you?

YJW 4: It [a knife] is something that they will just pick up, as if I would pick up a pair of headphones to go out. If they're going out, they'll just pick up a knife. It's so normal to them.

Unfortunately, justice-involved young people do not appear to fully appreciate the risks associated with carrying a knife, for example in relation to being an unintended perpetrator or victim of a stabbing, as a situation they find themselves in might quickly escalate. In the first six-part story (see Figure 4.1), Paul's intended victim, Jack, did not hand over his phone as requested. The situation quickly escalated to a point where Paul ended up stabbing his victim in the head.

As demonstrated in the quotes below, this inability to think through the implications of carrying a knife was also highlighted by a number of the workers. In their experience, young people do not fully appreciate the risks associated with carrying a knife, not only of becoming a perpetrator and/or victim of a stabbing, but also of being stopped and searched by the police and being found in possession of a weapon. As the final quote below highlights, this is often the case in instances of child criminal exploitation; an issue that will be discussed in more detail later, in Chapter 6.

YJW 5:   They don't think past carrying that knife ... In their head, it's just there for self-defence ... "I want to make sure that I've got one in case someone pulls one out on me. It might scare them off and then everything will be okay." They don't see past that pulling out of the knife.

YJW 10: I've had a few young people through that have been carrying knives ... They've had the knife for protection, but they haven't recognized ... the implications of carrying a knife and the risk that it carries for them.

YJW 4:   Often, if you're being criminally exploited, the exploiters will tell you to carry a weapon in case anything goes wrong. So, I have had kids disclose that [they] have been given a machete and ... the drugs to sell. It [the knife] would [be]come part and parcel ... [But] when kids are getting stop [and] searched, they [the police] are finding drugs and weapons together.

Figure 4.1: Excerpt from Story 1

The lack of consequential thinking was also discussed by the young people in both of the participatory workshops. They spoke of an "in the moment" mentality towards SYV, which is a common feature in psychodynamic explanations for violence (Yakeley 2018), where an inability to think empathically and rationally within a given situation can lead to incidences of spontaneous and destructive violence (Fonagy and Target 1995). Indeed, the young people in the second workshop talked of how "you don't think about" the consequences at the time of the offence. This was reflected in the first workshop when the young people were discussing why Paul stabbed Jack:

> It [the stabbing of Jack] happened on impulse. People either go for it or don't go for it, but if you're going to have a fight, be 100 per cent in it. Paul didn't think it through at the time, that came later. He thinks about the consequences now, but it's after [the stabbing] and that's the regret.

In addition to the issue of "regret", the young people in the first workshop talked of Paul worrying about reprisals following his stabbing of Jack. They said how he would be feeling "paranoid", "consumed by fear" and "alert all of the time". The issue of reprisals was also discussed in the second workshop. It was felt that perpetrating a SYV offence, particularly a stabbing, made it highly likely that you would be stabbed yourself at some point; which they saw as reinforcing the need to carry a knife. As one of the young people noted:

> If you stab someone, it's likely that it's going to happen to you. It might not happen the next day or the next week, but at some point in your life, it's probably going to end up coming back on to you. That's why most people nowadays will get about with a knife.

FIVE

Adverse Childhood Experiences

Prevalence of adverse childhood experiences

When compared to young people in general, those entering the justice system are much more likely to have experienced childhood adversity. As outlined in Chapter 2, studies in both the USA (Duke et al 2010; Dierkhising et al 2013; Baglivio et al 2014; Fox et al 2015) and the UK (Boswell 1996; Jacobson et al 2010; Her Majesty's Inspectorate of Probation 2017; Martin et al 2021) have consistently shown that adverse childhood experiences (ACEs) are disproportionally prevalent among young people involved in the justice system. For example, Martin et al (2021) found that young people entering the secure estate were twice as likely as young people in the general population to have experienced one or more ACEs, and over 13 times more likely to have experienced four or more. With this in mind, it was unsurprising that all of the youth justice workers interviewed for this research noted the high prevalence of ACEs among the young people they work with. They noted how rare it was for the assessment tool (see Figure 3.1) to show only one or two of the ten ACEs, with most young people assessed having many more:

| Youth justice worker [YJW] 6: | Looking at my cases, … most of them have more than four or five individual traumas. |
| YJW 5: | I think I've had one [young person] with two [ACEs], but that's it. The rest of them are quite high, sixes and sevens. |

YJW 10:   All my young people ... have experienced ACEs. All of them have had at least eight or more.

The interview findings were supported by the data collected using the ACEs assessment tool. As can be seen in Figure 5.1, over three quarters (78 per cent, n=155) of the young people who were assessed had an ACE score of four or more. Indeed, over a fifth (22 per cent, n=43) had a score of eight or more, and three young people had all ten ACEs. Only two of the young people assessed had no recorded ACEs. The average ACE score for the sample was 5.38, with a standard deviation of 2.41. While this is slightly lower than the average score of 5.55 found by Martin et al (2021), it needs to be remembered that the study by Martin et al focussed on young people in the secure estate who had committed more serious offences than the young people in this research, who were all serving community sentences. This might also account for the finding that over four fifths of their sample had an ACE score of four or more (Martin et al 2021).

When considering the findings from the ACEs assessment tool, it is important to consider the cumulative effect of ACEs. It was noted in Chapter 2 that, as ACE scores increase, the mean

Figure 5.1: Number of ACEs (n=200)

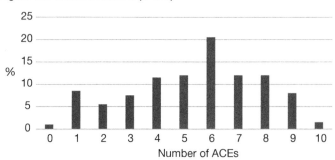

number of life-course convictions also tends to increase (Craig et al 2017a). And when it comes to violence in particular, it has been found that each additional ACE significantly increases the risk that violence will be perpetrated (Duke et al 2010). Indeed, a higher ACE score significantly increases the chances of a young person being classified as a serious violent offender (Perez et al 2018), as well as the likelihood of a young person committing a violent offence against multiple victim groups (Baglivio et al 2021). Furthermore, the accumulation of multiple ACEs has also been shown to be responsible for the association between ACEs and mental health problems in justice-involved young people, with each additional ACE exponentially increasing the risk of a young person developing mental health problems (Fox et al 2015; Perez et al 2018; Turner et al 2021).

Notwithstanding the high prevalence of ACEs identified among this cohort of justice-involved young people, it is likely that this is an under-estimation of the actual number of ACEs that the young people had lived through. As Asmussen et al (2020: 8) note, official statistics on the prevalence of ACEs only reflect the 'tip of the iceberg, since the majority of child maltreatment cases go unreported'. Often this is the result of under-reporting by parents/carers or under-detection by official agencies (Reuben et al 2016). Indeed, although Boswell (1996) and Jacobson et al (2010) found a high prevalence of ACEs among young people serving custodial sentences, both studies included the caveat that, due to being based on officially recorded data, their findings were likely to be significant under-estimates. Additionally, the validity of studies that retrospectively measure adults' recollections of childhood adversity has been questioned because of the potential for bias and misclassification (Reuben et al 2016).

It was to address some of these issues that the ACEs tool adopted for this piece of research was a 'live' document that could be updated as and when a youth justice worker found out more information about a young person (see Chapter 3). However, despite this, a number of the workers who were interviewed felt that the prevalence of ACEs identified by the ACEs tool was still an under-estimate of the actual number of ACEs that the young people had lived through. This was largely owing to the worry that what young people disclosed to their youth justice worker was just the "tip of the iceberg", and that actually there was much adversity that they chose not to disclose. The reasons for a young person choosing not to disclose their ACEs is an important issue that will be discussed in more detail in Chapter 7.

YJW 6: I think we're just scratching the tip of the iceberg ... We only know about what [ACEs] they tell us about, and that really worries me.

YJW 2: The sad thing is, ... what we know of [in terms of ACEs] we know from records ... or even what the young person might be telling us. [But] it's the tip of the iceberg. There's so much buried down that they're not going to talk to us about, that we don't know about, that might have gone on hidden before services became involved.

Before moving on to look at the types of ACE that were identified by the ACEs assessment tool, it is worth noting that, alongside the high prevalence of ACEs that were identified, there also appeared to be a dearth of positive influences in the young people's lives. For example, when the young people who were interviewed using the McAdams approach (see Chapter 3) were asked to talk about "the single person, group or organization that has had the greatest positive influence on your life story", four of the nine young people could not identify a single positive influence in their lives:

Young person [YP] 6:   I don't think that there has been one, to be honest.

Similarly, when the young people were asked to "describe a scene or a moment in your life that stands out as being especially positive, a really good moment for you", three of the young people were not able to recall any previous or current positive moments:

YP 3:	There isn't really one.
Interviewer [I]:	There must be some good moments in there …
YP 3:	I can't think of any.
YP 7:	I don't know really … I can't think of much.
I:	Is there something that you're doing in your life at the moment that gives you a sense of happiness?
YP 7:	Not right now, no.
YP 5:	Not really. Something happens every so often, every year at least.
I:	What do you mean by something happens?
YP 5:	Some shit. Can't I just have a year where nothing happens and it's just a good year?

Types of adverse childhood experiences

When it comes to the types of ACE that were identified using the ACEs tool, Figure 5.2 shows that, out of the ten ACEs that were assessed, the one that was most commonly identified was 'parental separation/loss'. This ACE was identified in over four fifths (84 per cent, n=167) of the young people in this research. The prevalence of parental separation and/or loss through bereavement is a frequently occurring ACE among justice-involved young people. For example, Martin et al (2021)

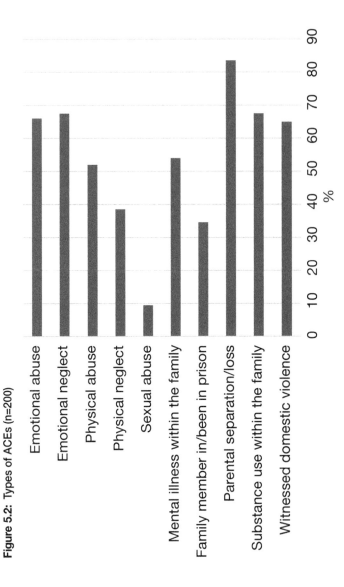

Figure 5.2: Types of ACEs (n=200)

found that parental separation was one of the most commonly identified ACEs in their study, and likewise, a Her Majesty's Inspectorate of Probation (2017) inspection found that separation from parents and/or the death of a parent or main carer was frequently identified. Boswell (1996) also found that 57 per cent of the 200 young people in her study had experienced significant parental loss of contact or bereavement. While this figure is lower than the 84 per cent stated above, as previously mentioned the fact that Boswell's study relied solely on officially recorded data makes it likely that her figure was an under-estimate. Added to this, Boswell's focus on loss of contact or bereavement excluded parental separation, which is likely to be more common.

In addition to the finding from the ACEs assessment tool, parental separation and/or loss was also highlighted by both the workers and the young people who were interviewed. Furthermore, during the third participatory workshop, when the childhood experiences of those who become involved in serious youth violence (SYV) were being discussed, experiencing 'parental separation/loss' was ranked as the second most common experience (see Table 3.7).

YJW 4: There's a lot of parental separation. I think that is really high. Yes, I'd say that is probably the highest.
I: Thinking back over your entire life, please identify a scene that stands out as a low point.
YP 3: My dad ... left and then came back, and then left [again]. I [last] spoke to him when I was 13. He said that he didn't want me. That's what he said, he didn't want to talk to me. That was the last time [I spoke to him].
I: Thinking back over your entire life, please identify a scene that stands out as a low point.
YP 9: When my mum and dad split up when I was young, 8 or 9. I didn't understand. It happened so fast. I didn't have a choice who I was going to live with. They didn't sit me down and talk about it.

> We just moved ... [and] I was in a new house with
> my mum and her new partner. I found it hard to
> sleep at night because I was thinking about it.

In line with other studies (Her Majesty's Inspectorate of
Probation 2017), 'substance use within the family' was another
commonly identified ACE, with just over two thirds (68 per
cent, n=135) of the assessed young people having experienced
it. Indeed, one of the youth justice workers noted how
"substance misuse amongst the family is massive" (YJW 4).
In the third participatory workshop, when the ACEs of those
who become involved in SYV were ranked, 'familial substance
use' came third (see Table 3.7).

I: Can you think of a single person or a group or
          an organization that's had the greatest negative
          influence on your life?
YP 3:   My stepdad ... Growing up, he started being a
          problem because he was always drinking and that ...
          I'd come home from school and he was sat there
          drunk, ... doing my head in [and] saying stuff to
          me that really got under my skin.

In line with research in the secure estate (Martin et al 2021),
two thirds (66 per cent, n=132) of the assessed young people
had experienced 'emotional abuse'. Alongside this, over two
thirds (68 per cent, n=135) had experienced 'emotional
neglect', and over half (56 per cent, n=111) had experienced
both 'emotional neglect' and 'emotional abuse':

YJW 2: When I did the [ACEs] screening for my caseload,
        I think every single one had emotional abuse
        and neglect.

While not as commonly identified as emotional abuse or
neglect, just over half (52 per cent, n=104) of the assessed

young people had experienced 'physical abuse'. This is important when one bears in mind that physical abuse is one of the ACEs that is most strongly associated with violent and aggressive offending in adolescence (Braga et al 2017). Alongside physical abuse, and in line with other research investigating the prevalence of ACEs among young people in the secure estate (Martin et al 2021), around two fifths (39 per cent, n=77) of the assessed young people had experienced 'physical neglect'.

When it comes to abuse in general (emotional, physical and/ or sexual), exactly three quarters (75 per cent, n=150) of the assessed young people had experienced some form of abuse. These abuse ACEs often cluster together. For example, if a young person has experienced physical abuse, then there is a greater chance that they will have also experienced emotional abuse (Asmussen et al 2020). Significantly, when it comes to SYV, Maas et al (2008) found that when these types of abuse ACEs are compounded, the likelihood that violence will be or has been perpetrated increases.

In terms of general neglect, over seven tenths (71 per cent, n=142) of the assessed young people had experienced some form of neglect (emotional and/or physical). Shockingly, three fifths (60 per cent, n=121) of the young people had experienced *both* some form of abuse *and* neglect. While this is a lower percentage than that found in Boswell's (1996) research, where just under three-quarters of the sample had experienced some form of abuse and neglect, it should be remembered that her research focussed on young people in the secure estate who had committed more serious offences than the young people in this research, who were all serving community sentences. Bearing in mind that each additional ACE significantly increases the likelihood that a young person will commit an offence serious enough to warrant a custodial sentence (Perez et al 2018), it might be expected that those young people serving custodial sentences will have experienced more abuse and neglect than those serving community sentences.

Of the 200 young people who were assessed using the ACEs tool, just over half (55 per cent, n=109) had experienced what Boswell (1996: 91) refers to as the 'double childhood trauma' of parental separation/loss *and* abuse/neglect. While this is higher than the 35 per cent that Boswell found in her study, as previously mentioned she relied solely on officially recorded data and thus it is likely that her figure is an under-estimate.

The other ACE that was identified in nearly two thirds (65 per cent, n=130) of the assessed young people was 'witnessed domestic violence'. Again, mindful of the issue of official under-reporting, this is much higher than that found in a Prison Reform Trust study where 28 per cent had witnessed domestic violence (Jacobson et al 2010). It is also much higher than a Her Majesty's Inspectorate of Probation (2017) inspection that found that one third of young people who had committed a violent offence had grown up in a household where there was a formal record of domestic violence.

Interestingly, 'witnessed domestic violence' was often identified alongside 'physical abuse'. Indeed, nearly two thirds (65 per cent, n=85) of young people who had 'witnessed domestic violence' had also been victims of 'physical abuse'. As Asmussen et al (2020) found, owing to the clustering of particular ACEs, young people who have experienced physical abuse are more likely to have witnessed domestic violence as well. This is significant when one bears in mind that research has shown that witnessing and/or experiencing domestic violence can have long-lasting effects on young people's predisposition to engage in violence (Weaver et al 2008). Furthermore, other studies (Vaughn et al 2014; Williams et al 2018; Criminal Justice Joint Inspection 2021) have found that those who grow up in households that are characterized by violence and physical abuse are more likely to have a history of violent victimization and resulting traumatic brain injury (TBI), which itself has been shown to be associated with impulsive violence and aggression (Williams et al 2018).

The high prevalence of domestic violence among justice-involved young people was identified by all of the workers and therapists that were interviewed:

Drama therapist [DT] 2:	A lot of the time, the first thing that I'll pick up on is there's been domestic violence. You can almost pretty much guarantee it at youth justice.
YJW 6:	Witnessing domestic violence ... [and] being exposed to violence themselves ... are probably the most common ones [ACEs] that I come across.
YJW 5:	The majority of them have domestic violence at home. They've either witnessed it or experienced it ... There's a lot of that kind of violence going on.

During the third participatory workshop, 'witnessing domestic violence' was ranked as the most common ACE of those who become involved in SYV (see Table 3.7). Indeed, during the creation of the six-part story in the first workshop (see Figure 3.2), domestic violence featured heavily in the life of the perpetrator Paul:

Paul was a very happy child and then in Year 5 everything went pear-shaped. His dad had an affair and is inflicting domestic violence on his mum. Paul sees everything at home. He sits at the top of the stairs. He feels weak, helpless and everything is getting worse ... Paul is traumatized by his childhood experiences ... He wasn't ready for it. No one's ready for that, witnessing the fighting between parents. He thinks that the world is shit and he's given up. He knows that running from home is creating other problems and he's trying very hard, but survival is fight or flight.

Despite not being asked for on the ACEs assessment tool, a number of the workers felt that poverty and deprivation had played a key role in some young people's offending behaviour, and that socio-economic deprivation was a significant ACE for some of the young people they had worked with. As mentioned in Chapter 1, it is worth remembering that in 2019 Manchester ranked as the sixth most deprived local authority in England (Ministry of Housing, Communities and Local Government 2019) and, at the start of 2022, around one in four young people in the city were living in poverty (Greater Manchester Poverty Action 2022).

In line with research that has found a relationship between ACEs and socio-economic deprivation (Walsh et al 2019), the quotes below clearly illustrate how poverty played a role in some young people's offending behaviour. As noted in the Youth Violence Commission's final report (Irwin-Rogers et al 2020), growing up in poverty can lead young people to feel rejected by society. This rejection can elicit feelings of shame and humiliation, which in turn trigger feelings of anger; anger which often manifests itself in violence (Thomas 1995; Gilligan 2003). The role of shame and humiliation in the perpetration of SYV offences will be discussed in more depth in Chapter 6.

YJW 9:   Mum has barely any money to support him and his reason [for committing SYV offences] when I first interviewed him was "I don't want to stress my mum out and ask for money. I just figured that … this was a way for me to earn money on my own" … Obviously it wasn't right, but we need to think about the positions that these young people are in, the choices that they make.

DT 2:   One young man, … mum lost her job, they had no money, and she couldn't wash their clothes because she had no money to get washing-up stuff, and she just broke down. I remember him saying, "My mum broke down because we had no money, and I'd never seen my mum break down before. And something clicked in me and I said, 'This is enough'. I just got so angry at why this was happening to us, and I just went out and I stole a phone off somebody, and it was really easy, and that was it, it just snowballed, and I just stole loads of stuff." Yes, I think they get pushed to the limit and they break.

Interestingly, during the second participatory workshop the young participants talked of young people "out there doing stuff 'cos they haven't got food on the table and stuff like that". Indeed, they felt that these young people "actually have a reason" to be committing SYV offences. Money also featured heavily in the six-part stories that were created during the first and second workshops. In the first workshop, the young people talked of Paul "buzzing" at the thought of making £2,000, while in the second workshop, the young people talked of James offering two random people £10,000 each to help kidnap and assault Joe, the victim in the story (see Figure 5.3).

When it came to the third workshop, the theme of "money" was ranked as the number one reason why young people might become involved in perpetrating SYV offences (see Table 3.5). The considerable amounts of money that young people can make from illicit activities is often a draw that is hard to resist, particularly for those young people living in poverty (Irwin-Rogers 2019). At the same time, though, these activities significantly increase the likelihood of young people becoming involved in SYV, both as a perpetrator and/or a victim. The allure of money and its relationship to child criminal exploitation and SYV will be returned to in Chapter 6.

Using the ACEs assessment tool

Before moving on to discuss the relationship between ACEs and SYV, it is worth briefly touching on the youth

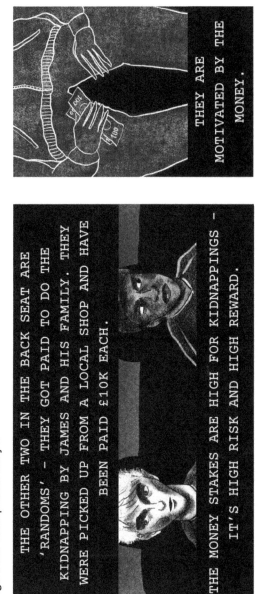

Figure 5.3: Excerpt from Story 2

justice workers' views of the ACEs assessment tool and their experiences of using it in their everyday practice. Since 2014, all youth justice services in England and Wales have used AssetPlus, an integrated assessment and planning framework that was designed to help youth justice workers assess and plan interventions for the young people they work with (Baker 2012; Youth Justice Board 2014). Yet despite AssetPlus having an explicit focus on assessing a young person's risk of reoffending alongside their needs, the youth justice workers and therapists that were interviewed unanimously agreed that the ACEs assessment tool was particularly useful when it came to identifying a young person's ACEs. As one worker noted, it is "good to see it quantified" (YJW 6). Furthermore, and in line with a trauma-informed approach, some of the workers felt that the tool helped them to better understand a young person's behaviour and individual needs:

I: Do you think it's a useful tool?
DT 2:   Yes, I do ... I think it creates an awareness and a better understanding of behaviour.
I: How are you finding using the ACEs tool?
YJW 5: I find it keeps my head in a space of thinking of what the child might have experienced, before I start thinking about what we can do ... I actually look at each [ACE] and think "are we addressing that or is somebody [else] addressing that?" while I'm making the plan. I find it really useful.
I: How have you found using the ACEs screening tool?
YJW 9: The screening tool is so helpful because, even though I knew that my young people had been through trauma, actually putting it in and going "he's got seven ACEs, ... that's a lot of things going on that I really need to take that into account" ... I'm like "I need to be aware of all these complex things working together to help this young person more."

SIX

The Relationship between Adverse Childhood Experiences and Serious Youth Violence

> When you're looking at serious youth violence ... you've got to understand where it comes from, how it comes about, and how it manifests.
>
> (Youth justice worker [YJW] 2)

The preceding two chapters have outlined the prevalence and nature of adverse childhood experiences (ACEs) and serious youth violence (SYV) among justice-involved young people in Manchester. This chapter now moves on to investigate the complex relationship between ACEs and SYV. It looks at the impact of ACEs on a young person's mind and body, as well as their identity formation. It finishes with a discussion of the relevance of attachment theory to an investigation of the relationship between ACEs and SYV.

Before doing this, however, it is important to note that not everyone who experiences ACEs has a negative outcome (McCartan 2020). While exposure to childhood adversity significantly increases the likelihood of offending later in life, the link between ACEs and later violent behaviour is far from certain, since a large portion of abused and neglected young people do not go on to a life of crime (Widom 1989). Nonetheless, ACEs have been found to be strongly associated with a range of 'problematic behaviours' including aggression, violence and criminal behaviour (Liddle et al 2016).

Impact on the mind

To properly comprehend the relationship between ACEs and the violent behaviour of justice-involved young people, it is important to understand the impact of ACEs on a psychological level. Herman (2015) was the first to use the term 'complex trauma' to describe a constellation of symptoms that occur following chronic, repetitive or prolonged exposure to traumatic experiences. Building upon theories of post-traumatic stress disorder (PTSD), Herman describes how 'complex trauma' can produce similar effects and symptoms to PTSD, including for example affect dysregulation, dissociation and identity disturbance. These symptoms are commonly over-represented in those who have experienced, for example, domestic violence or childhood abuse (Herman 2015). The *Eleventh Revision of The International Classification of Diseases* (World Health Organization 2022) describes complex trauma as having three main elements: re-experiencing the traumatic event/s in the present, avoidance of these intrusions and an excessive sense of current threat.

From a psychotherapeutic point of view, ACEs can be thought of as piercing the protective shield around the mind (Freud 1920). This can be psychologically damaging because when an element of reality evokes too much anxiety, an internal psychic defence is established to help deny, avoid or manage any anxieties. If the anxieties are too powerful to be managed or worked off in the normal way, a young person can feel psychologically overwhelmed and psychological disturbances can result (Freud 1916). In the field of psychotherapy, there is a growing recognition of the role of ACEs and childhood trauma in the development of multiple diagnoses, including for example personality disorders, dissociation, depression, anxiety and psychosis (Stubley and Young 2022). Added to this, traumatized individuals can demonstrate disturbances in emotional regulation. This can result in behavioural disturbances, such as self-destructive acts and violent behaviour, or disturbances in self-concept and identity, which can create feelings of shame, guilt, failure and worthlessness (Gilligan 1996). ACEs experienced during adolescence can also reactivate anxieties from early childhood, resulting in a young person feeling lost, abandoned and/or persecuted (Hinshelwood 1989).

Within the present research, every single one of the youth justice workers who was interviewed felt that ACEs have a detrimental impact on the emotional well-being of the young people they work with. While some of the workers talked of how being continually exposed to ACEs had affected the mental health of the young people they work with, others discussed the impact of ACEs on how well the young people were able to manage their emotions. Both of these points are supported by research that has investigated the effects of ACEs on mental health and emotional well-being. For example, Fox et al (2015) found that, while single ACEs did not necessarily increase the likelihood of developing mental health problems, the accumulation of multiple, different forms of ACEs was responsible for the association between ACEs and mental health problems evident in justice-involved young people. As evidenced in Chapter 5, the fact that the majority of the young people who were assessed had experienced multiple ACEs is significant when one bears in mind that research has found that each additional type of ACE exponentially increases the likelihood of developing mental health problems (Fox et al 2015; Perez et al 2018; Turner et al 2021).

YJW 5: I never knew that some kids lived in such chaos. Their lives are anxious [and] stressful. They wake up stressed [and] they go to bed stressed. There's no sense of peace for them ... It doesn't surprise me that having ACEs has an effect on their mental health.

YJW 2: When you've got that layer after layer, you know, poly-trauma, ... it just disrupts your thinking processes completely.

| YJW 4: | It [ACE] changes you from such a young age. It changes your way of thinking [and] it changes how you handle your emotions. |

In line with research that has investigated the relationship between ACEs, emotional regulation and externalized violent behaviour (Gilligan 1996; Turner et al 2021), the interviewees in this study reported multiple cases of young people who had experienced ACEs struggling to manage their emotions. As the quotes below demonstrate, this can manifest as anger and aggression in some young people.

Drama therapist [DT] 2:	Their emotions are so blurred. They're all confused, and it all seems to come out as anger or aggression because they can't recognize what it is that they're feeling.
Young person [YP] 5:	I had my nan's funeral and then two days after, this shit [the SYV offence] happened ... Shittiest week ever.
Interviewer [I]:	Do you think that your nan passing away impacted your behaviour?
YP 5:	It could have done because I was angry with everyone [and] I was losing my shit with everyone because my mind was just fucking, I don't even know what was up with my brain.

As discussed, ACEs can have a profound effect on a young person's mental health and emotional well-being, with those who have lived through childhood adversity struggling with a confusing mixture of feelings ranging from depression and shame, to anger and aggression (Gilligan 1996; Garland 1998). This is particularly the case for those young people who have witnessed domestic violence. Research has found that the psychological outcomes of young people who have witnessed domestic violence are significantly worse than those young people who have not (Herman 2015). And while the impact of witnessing domestic violence can vary for different individuals, it has been shown to have a particular negative impact on young people (Curran 2013). Young people have been found to exhibit an array of behaviours when coping with witnessing domestic violence, including externalized behaviours such as aggressiveness and violence, and internalized behaviours such as anxiety and depression (Meltzer et al 2009).

Alongside witnessing domestic violence, being a victim of physical abuse is another ACE that can engender the feelings outlined above. Evidence suggests that young people who are exposed to violence, either as a witness to domestic violence or as a victim of physical abuse, externalize and internalize problematic behaviours more highly in adolescence than those exposed to neither of these ACEs. Unsurprisingly, those who have experienced both of these ACEs are more likely to exhibit these problematic behaviours (Moylan et al 2010). This is significant because, as found in Chapter 5, witnessing domestic violence was one of the most commonly identified ACEs, and nearly two thirds (65 per cent, n=85) of those who had witnessed it had also been victims of 'physical abuse'.

From a psychotherapeutic perspective, ACEs can cause the distinction between a young person's inner world and the external world to collapse (Fonagy and Target 1996). As a result, the external world becomes a direct reflection of that young person's worst experiences and the accompanying fear and anxieties become reactivated. When a young person has witnessed and/or experienced pervasive violence and abuse in their childhood, their ability to 'reality check' becomes hampered, and their persecutory thoughts merge with external reality. This is dangerous because, once they lose the ability to regulate and reflect, their thinking and perception can become fixed and persecutory. This feeling of persecution can result in a young person feeling unsafe, with the threat of violence omnipresent.

DT 1:   A lot of my young people ... will talk about ... a sense of not being safe ... There is always that threat around them.

Research (Brennan and Moore 2009; Riggs and Palasinski 2011; Traynor 2016) has found that young people often start carrying knives as a defensive response to perceived threats. In line with this, several of the workers who were interviewed felt that the need to feel safe was directly linked to young people carrying knives and/or other weapons (see Chapter 4):

YJW 2:   If violence has been dominant in your childhood, then you can completely understand why people feel like they need to protect themselves.
YJW 8:   There's a reason why they are carrying knives ... A kid must have suffered some form of trauma, or some form of threat, for them to want to carry a knife.

Impact on the body

In addition to the psychological impact of ACEs is the physiological impact. As mentioned in Chapter 2, research has found a relationship between exposure to ACEs and impaired neurodevelopment (SAMHSA 2014), with ACEs increasing the chances of a young person having multiple neurodevelopmental disorders (NDD) (Dinkler et al 2017; Kirby 2021). This is especially the case in relation to attention deficit hyperactivity disorder (ADHD) and speech and language difficulties (Kirby 2021). Among justice-involved young people, ADHD has been found to be associated with violent offending (Cleaton and Kirby 2018) and an increased risk of child criminal exploitation (CCE) (Kirby et al 2020).

Also, justice-involved young people with ACEs frequently have a history of traumatic brain injury (TBI) alongside other NDDs, with rates of TBI ranging from one in six to nearly three in four (Kirby et al 2020). TBI appears to be linked to greater likelihood of violent victimization (Vaughn et al 2014; Williams et al 2018). The high prevalence of TBI among justice-involved young people is particularly relevant to this research because TBI has been found to be associated with higher impulsivity (Vaughn et al 2014), impulsive aggression, poor decision-making and lack of control of social behaviour (Williams et al 2018). All this considered, the neurodevelopmental research on ACEs, NDDs and TBI points to a significant reduction in the ability of justice-involved young people to judge a perceived threat and respond appropriately. This is important because, as Kirby (2021) argues, what is sorely lacking in the justice system's response to SYV is a better understanding of the neuroscience of ACEs, and the recognition that some justice-involved young people have to manage an over-active threat system grounded in neurodevelopmental conditions.

In his seminal book *The Body Keeps the Score*, Van der Kolk (2014) describes how ACEs can somatize: the body literally keeps the score. For example, it has been observed that many young people who have experienced ACEs display reduced activation in the ventromedial prefrontal cortex, which is the area in the brain that governs emotional regulation, reflexivity and displays of empathy (Mehta et al 2009). It has also been found that the hippocampus – the area of the brain responsible for forming memories and for memory retrieval – is reduced in many of those who have experienced ACEs (Anderson et al 2008). This is important because it means that those young people who have experienced ACEs often find it much harder to contextualize against other memories and learn from previous experiences.

Another physical manifestation of ACEs can be found in the 'fight-or-flight' response. This primitive survival response to potentially life-threatening situations is neurological in nature and is registered in the limbic system of the brain where the amygdala lies. The amygdala is a section of the brain that dictates the fight-or-flight response and registers potential threats. Van der Kolk (2014) compares the amygdala to a smoke alarm, constantly scanning for any potential fires to trigger the alarm and signify danger. The fight-or-flight response facilitates immediate action and can be experienced in the body as rapid breathing, trembling, dilated pupils, and changes in skin tone. These effects are part of the sympathetic and autonomic nervous systems which release adrenaline and cortisol. As Anda et al (2006) note, the fight-or-flight response among young people exposed to ACEs, and the attendant release of hormones, are both uncontrollable and invisible.

Evidence suggests that consistently having the fight-or-flight response triggered by ACEs can have a lasting, damaging impact on the developing brain (Stubley and Young, 2022) For example, it has been shown to have a detrimental effect on developing neural networks and on the neuroendocrine systems that regulate them (Anda et al 2006). Furthermore, the release of hormones triggered by the fight-or-flight response can result in a young person having difficulty expressing and controlling their emotions (Lubit et al 2003). Work by Palombo et al (2016) found that constant exposure to ACEs can stimulate the amygdala to constantly scan for danger. This can result in young people who have experienced ACEs being hypervigilant for threats and in a heightened state of chronic threat (Overstreet and Braun 2000; SAMHSA 2014), even when no threats are present (Teicher 2002; Van der Kolk 2014; Perry and Szalavitz 2007; Bath 2008). Indeed, several of the workers and drama therapists who were interviewed talked of the young people they work with being predominantly in the fight response to keep themselves feeling safe:

DT 1:   That trauma response is to fight, [fly] or freeze. The serious youth violence is those young people who have developed this real in-depth need to fight in order to keep themselves safe and to survive.

The notion of fight-or-flight was also evident in the six-part story from the first participatory workshop, when the young people talked of the domestic violence that the perpetrator Paul had witnessed and how, for him, "survival is fight or flight" (see Chapter 5). The notion that 'each danger signal is potentially felt to be extreme and requires a full stress response in return' (Stubley 2022a: 16) can help to explain why some young people who have experienced ACEs react in extreme ways to what they might perceive as a threat. According to Garland (1998), there are two types of anxiety: signal anxiety, which is experienced when danger threatens the individual, and automatic anxiety, which is experienced in situations of actual danger. A young person who has lived through ACEs is more likely to face situations that they perceive to be dangerous with a heightened sense of threat, and interpret subtle perceptions of danger (that is, tones of voice, facial expressions and so on) as threatening. These perceived threats may trigger a full-scale fight response because of automatic anxiety. When this triggering occurs, the higher executive functioning of the brain that governs rationality, organized thinking and regulation becomes disrupted and instead a defensive response is launched against the perceived threat.

The need to belong

Additional to the impact that ACEs can have on a young person's mind and body is the impact they can have on that person's identity formation. For some young people, the central developmental task of identity formation and separation into adulthood can be fundamentally skewed by ACEs (Stubley and Young 2022). ACEs can profoundly influence identificatory processes; so much so, that trauma becomes deeply embedded within the young person's sense of self and can therefore become detrimental to a more fluid identity formation. Adolescence is already fraught with the vicissitudes of identity development and these, when combined with inherent trauma, can cause problems for a young person. For example, research has shown that traumatized young people lack a sense of self-worth (Lubit et al 2003). Combined with this, during adolescence peer relationships grow in importance and can act as a crucial source of support and protection for young people (Firmin and Knowles 2020). This can be problematic if a young person's home life is devoid of the necessary support and protection, and they become over-reliant on gaining this from peers. As the youth justice workers who were interviewed noted, ACEs can lead to young people seeking out opportunities or behaving in particular ways that gain them praise and/or acceptance from their peers. Indeed, higher ACE scores have been found to be directly predictive of a young person's level of admiration and imitation of their deviant peers (Perez et al 2018), with those who are socially deprived more easily 'pressured to commit violent acts ... to be accepted by and to demonstrate commitment' to their peers (Baumeister and Leary 1995: 521).

YJW 10: If you're not accepted within your family or you've experienced a lot of abuse or neglect or negativity, you're going to want to do something that's going to make you be accepted by somebody else.

YJW 5: A lot of our young people don't get positive feedback from parents. They get a lot of shouting, a lot of arguments, ... [but] they don't get that praise. Their peers will praise them, but it's not necessarily for doing good things.

YJW 10: If you're suffering trauma, loss, rejection, fear, [then] you're going to want to find a group that's going to accept you, and you're also going to want to do stuff ... which will make you be more accepted by that group.

Research on belonging has shown that people are 'fundamentally and pervasively motivated by a need to belong' (Baumeister and Leary 1995: 522). This makes those young people who have experienced multiple ACEs more likely to be involved with gangs. Wolff et al (2020) found that cumulative trauma, as measured by an ACE score, represents a significant risk factor when it comes to gang involvement, largely because gang membership can provide a sense of belonging and bolster low self-esteem and self-worth (Hughes et al 2015a). Nearly all the workers who were interviewed felt that, in addition to commitment to deviant peer groups and/or gangs, the need to feel belonging and acceptance can make young people with multiple ACEs particularly susceptible to becoming victims of CCE:

YJW 4: A lot of our young people are seeking relationships elsewhere because they're not getting what they need at home ... Unfortunately, the exploiters pick up on that and give them what they've always wanted.

YJW 1: The majority of the young people that we come across are all very vulnerable ... and they're all at risk of being exploited, some more than others.

Bearing in mind the points made above, it is perhaps unsurprising that many of the workers talked of the young people they work with describing those that exploit them as family. As one worker described, exploiters are often talked about as "my brothers, ... my family on the road" (YJW 4). As highlighted in the quotes below, young people often viewed their exploiters as someone who was "always there" for them. Someone who would, for example, give them money for food:

YJW 4: They will talk about them [the exploiter] like they're an amazing role model. "They gave me this. They gave me that. They really care for me. They're always there for me."

I: Do you think there's a relationship between ACEs and CCE?

YJW 6: Yes, without a doubt ... When someone's offering you money and a sense of belonging it's a bit of a no-brainer ... That kid that I just mentioned, ... he was a 14-year-old who was involved in a gang manslaughter with older men. I said to him "the main guy that was involved in that, when you first saw him, what did you think of him?" And he said "I was scared. He was a really big scary man and he was standing there in the rain" – he described something out of a horror film – "but then he came up to me and said 'here you are kid, there's twenty quid to go and get yourself a bite and some chips' and I thought, yes, he's alright."

As the above quote highlights, the possibility of a real sense of belonging, combined with the prospect of financial gain and the concomitant status and respect, makes young people – particularly those who have multiple ACEs – vulnerable to exploitation. As one worker succinctly noted, "where we say exploitation, the vast majority of children are saying it's opportunity" (YJW 7). Unfortunately, as highlighted in Chapter 4, the outcome of the exploitation is that vulnerable young people often end up committing SYV offences:

DT 2:   These kids ... haven't got the family support ... They're seeking that family dynamic and they [the exploiters] are there: "We'll embrace you; we'll take you in. But go and do this first." And the kids will just do it.

The need to belong to someone or something is part of the human condition. Central to this need is the idea that one matters. Work by Elliot et al (2004: 339) has conceptualized mattering as the perception that we are a 'significant part of the world around us' which can help to defend against feelings of loss and insignificance. Alongside this, mattering is the belief that one makes a difference (Elliot et al 2004) which can increase feelings of self-worth and respect. Mattering, therefore, is the sense of being connected to others and having the agency to impact the world around you (Flett 2018; Prilleltensky 2020). From a psychotherapeutic point of view, it is important for individuals to perceive a sense of significance and power by feeling recognized and influential (May 1998). For those justice-involved young people with multiple ACEs, the inability to garner this through more traditional means (such as family, work, education) results in their finding alternative ways to feel significant and to make their mark on the world (for further discussion see Billingham and Irwin-Rogers 2022). Unfortunately, for these young people the search for significance and belonging often takes shape through connections fostered with their peers on the street and/or through the victimization of others to achieve a sense of power.

The relevance of attachment theory

Before moving on to look at trauma-informed practice, this chapter finishes with a brief discussion of the relevance and applicability of attachment theory to an investigation of the relationship between ACEs and SYV. Attachment theory looks at the importance of the developing brain on emotions and behaviours throughout the lifespan of an individual (Schaefer 2011). Rooted in a psychotherapeutic modality, attachment theory was developed by John Bowlby as a direct response to the issues of family separation and loss during the Second World War. Bowlby (1944; 1950) was one of the first to pioneer the idea that early forms of traumatic separation and loss can have a negative impact on adolescent behaviour. Because attachment theory gives us the ability to grasp the importance of the caregiver relationship and the effect that a poor or insecure attachment can have on subsequent behaviour, it can provide a useful lens to enhance our understanding of the drivers behind SYV.

Infants are genetically predisposed to want access and proximity to their caregiver, particularly when frightened (De Zulueta 2006). As infants depend totally on their caregiver (for food, shelter and safety), any threat to the infant's sense of safety and security activates the system of attachment to their caregiver (Bowlby 1980). This is because the infant is unable to regulate their emotional world and maintain psychological homeostasis without assistance. Hence, part of the role of the caregiver is to attend and be sensitive to their infant's distress by 'containing' any anxieties and reflecting back a calm and soothing emotional world (Bion 1963), what Stern (1985) refers to as 'affect attunement'. This attunement allows the infant to make sense and meaning of their distressing experiences and thereby develop 'internal working models' on which they can draw in later life (Bowlby 1988; Fonagy et al 1997). These particular infants have what Bowlby (1969) refers to as a 'secure base', an internal working model that feels safe and secure in times of need. In other words, the securely attached infant will have a good internal model of the caregiver as responsive and caring in times of need (Siegel 2001). In contrast, those who do not have a secure attachment, and lack a positive internal working model of a caregiver, are often referred to as insecurely attached (Bowlby 1988). When insecurely attached young people are confronted with anxieties or anxiety-evoking situations, to ensure their psychic survival they will evacuate their anxieties, often in the form of destructive behaviour such as violence (Minsky 1998). Indeed, as Parsons (2009: 369) notes, it is 'anxiety that leads to the pathological use of aggression and violence'.

We would argue that attachment theory is particularly relevant when looking at the relationship between ACEs and SYV. It provides a useful theoretical backdrop that can help us to better understand how ACEs are associated with violent behaviour in adolescence. This is not to suggest that every young person who experiences poor attachment in their early childhood will go onto perpetrate violence, but rather to recognize that those who were insecurely attached in childhood might be more likely to commit violent offences in adolescence. As Levinson and Fonagy (2004: 236) remind us, 'it is important to retain awareness of the possibility that violence may be rooted in the disorganization of the attachment system'. Young people who perpetrate violent acts tend to be those who were not enabled in childhood to develop a secure attachment in which they felt loved and contained, such as 'institutionalized children with multiple caretakers, traumatized children who have suffered severe physical pain, neglect or over-stimulation, and children for whom fear has been a daily currency' (Parsons 2009: 364). It is important to remember that of the 200 young people who were assessed in this study, over four fifths (84 per cent, n=167) had experienced 'parental separation/loss', exactly three quarters (75 per cent, n=150) had experienced some form of abuse (emotional, physical and/or sexual), over seven tenths (71 per cent, n=142) had experienced some form of neglect (emotional and/or physical) and three fifths (60 per cent, n=121) had experienced both abuse *and* neglect.

SEVEN

Trauma-informed Practice

There is that real balance within the youth justice [system] about understanding that we're working with victims as well as perpetrators, and we need to tackle both.

(Drama therapist [DT] 1)

As outlined in Chapter 2, from 2016 onwards there has been a growing awareness of the importance of delivering trauma-informed practice within a youth justice context (Liddle et al 2016; Cordis Bright 2017; Glendinning et al 2021). Bearing in mind the prevalence of adverse childhood experiences (ACEs) among justice-involved young people (see Chapter 5), and the complex relationship between ACEs and serious youth violence (SYV) (see Chapter 6), it is clear that a trauma-informed approach is essential when working with perpetrators of SYV. Yet despite this awareness, the actual delivery of trauma-informed practice with justice-involved young people can be challenging. Before moving on to discuss these challenges, however, this chapter will first outline the strengths of a trauma-informed approach.

Strengths of a trauma-informed approach

The Substance Abuse and Mental Health Services Administration (SAMHSA 2014) report that was drawn upon in Chapter 2 is arguably one of the most comprehensive documents relating to trauma-informed approaches and trauma-informed care. In addition to developing a robust concept of trauma and how it manifests in individuals, the report presents a viable framework for embedding trauma-informed practice into public health agencies and organizations, ranging from education to social care and criminal justice. According to SAMHSA, the concept of trauma-informed practice requires agencies and organizations to apply the principles of trauma-informed care to all areas of their functioning. Working in trauma-informed ways requires 'all people at all levels of the organization or system [to] have a basic realization about trauma and understand how trauma can affect families, groups, organizations, and communities as well as individuals' (SAMHSA 2014: 9). With this approach in mind, a young person's violent behaviour should be understood in the context of coping strategies designed to survive adversity and trauma, whether this occurred in the past or is occurring at present.

In line with this, when the youth justice workers were asked to give their understanding of the term trauma-informed practice, responses ranged from being able to recognize how ACEs might impact upon young people's "everyday lives and the way they react to things", through to how workers engage and work with traumatized young people:

Youth justice worker [YJW] 9:	It's being able to recognize the significant trauma that these young people have been through, and how much that will affect their everyday lives and the way that they react to things.
YJW 10:	It's having an understanding about why a young person does what they do ... It's also having an understanding of the impact that they [ACEs] have on the young person's development.

YJW 6:   We need to work on the assumption that bad things have happened ... and think about how you interact and communicate with [young] people based on that.

For the workers that were interviewed, the scope of a trauma-informed approach to increase the "understanding about why a young person does what they do" was felt to be the major strength of the approach. As one of the workers noted:

YJW 4:   Without understanding all of the trauma that these kids have been through, you can't explain why they've done what they've done, why they're here ... None of that [their offending] makes sense if you don't understand their experiences and their lives.

It was felt that it was only once a worker knew a "young person's whole story" that they could "come up with a bespoke intervention plan for them that fits their needs" (YJW 8). This desire for youth justice workers to better understand the reasons why a young person may have committed a crime was also highlighted in the participatory workshops. During the third participatory workshop, the themes "Someone to understand the reasons why you have committed the violent offence" and "Someone to understand your childhood experiences" were ranked as the second and third most important types of support that a justice-involved young person needs (see Table 3.8). Alongside this, it was felt that a trauma-informed approach, with its emphasis on better understanding what a young person has been through, helps to build trusted relationships between workers and young people, and thus facilitates the disclosure of ACEs. As evidenced below, this came out of both the worker interviews and the discussion in the first participatory workshop:

DT 2:	It [a trauma-informed approach] creates better relationships with the young people. It helps to build trust [and] I think the young people are more willing to come in and see the staff. There's just that better communication ... [which] I think does benefit the young person, very much so.
Interviewer [I]:	Do you think it makes it easier for young people to disclose their ACEs?
DT 2:	Yes ... It just creates that space for them to tell you about them.

Paul needed someone to understand his background and all of the things that he had experienced ... He wants people to know how it all started so that he can deal with it better ... Once working with the youth justice team, Paul received a lot of help from his YOT worker,[1] and they became the person he talked to. Paul liked that his worker knows what is going on in the house and is really understanding.

Working with justice-involved young people in this trauma-informed way maps directly onto the six principles that SAMHSA (2014) argue are fundamental to a trauma-informed approach.[2] While the principles are not prescriptive and can be generalized to different sectors, what is important is that services and organizations adopt a strengths–based model that prioritizes the person, while also recognizing both the trauma and the risk factors. As such, a trauma-informed approach with its emphasis on "what happened to you?" as opposed to "what's wrong with you?" closely aligns with a person first approach (McCartan 2020). With this in mind, it can be seen how working in a trauma-informed way dovetails with the Youth Justice Board's current focus on a strengths-based, Child First approach (Youth Justice Board 2021), as well as research that advocates the participation of justice-involved young people in decisions that affect them (Smithson et al 2021).

Barriers to delivering a trauma-informed approach

Notwithstanding the strengths of a trauma-informed approach and the calls to rethink how traumatized young people are supported (Ryan and Mitchell 2011; Rogers and Budd 2015), all of the youth justice workers who were interviewed for this research reported encountering a range of barriers when trying to implement trauma-informed practice. For example, even with the best support plan in place, the workers were fully aware that they could not "force" a young person to engage. This view was further supported by the young people in the second participatory workshop. As one of them noted, "until a person is ready [to engage] forget about it. They have to be ready to engage."

YJW 1: We can have a brilliant plan and support mechanisms ... in place for the young person, but it's only going to be effective if the young person engages with it.

YJW 8: There's only so much I can do ... It's up to them if they want the support. I can't force it on them. I can't tell them that they have to change. They need to want to make that change in their lives.

This issue of not being able to "force" young people to engage is even more evident when it comes to supporting a young person to disclose their ACEs. As one of the workers noted, "we only know about what [ACEs] they tell us about" (YJW 6) (see also Chapter 5). There are multiple reasons why a young person may choose to not disclose their ACEs. Research has shown that ACEs can lead to high rates of non-engagement because they tend to blunt young people's 'cognitive readiness' (Skuse and Matthew 2015: 22). ACEs can also result in a general lack of trust of adults (Garland 1998; Welfare and Hollin 2012; Wright et al 2016). Alongside this, it has been found that young people simply want to avoid thinking about, or discussing, painful experiences and events (Welfare and

Hollin 2012; Criterion C – American Psychiatric Association 2013; Gray 2015; Wright et al 2016), with justice-involved young men often wanting to present themselves as 'super-masculine' and invulnerable (Goff et al 2007: 156). Also, it is often the case that young people who have been exposed to physical abuse are threatened with violence if they disclose the abuse, resulting in them being too scared to reach out for help (SAMHSA 2014). Whatever the reason why a young person may choose not to disclose ACEs, the result is generally the same: an 'unwillingness or refusal to talk with staff about their ... history' (Welfare and Hollin 2012: 99). This was evidenced by both the young people and workers who were interviewed:

Young person [YP] 5:   I said I was fine and just denied everything.

I: Why did you deny everything?

YP 5:   I just didn't want to speak about everything.

I: Can you describe your biggest life challenge to date?

YP 6:   There have been a lot of challenges, not just one, [but] I don't talk about things like this. I usually keep them to myself. I would rather not say. I don't want to talk about the past ... I can't go there.

DT 2:   It's hard to talk about your trauma and hard to talk about things that have been done to you, and they don't always want to do it ... I think they'd rather be angry and shouting and have that confrontation, than feel exposed and vulnerable.

This reticence to disclose or discuss ACEs is not surprising when one considers the wider psychotherapeutic literature on trauma. As Garland (1998: 99) writes, trauma can result in the mind's 'protective shield' being breached, as well as overloading the mind's capacity to process and deal with external stimuli, including the many differing requirements of the various agencies and organizations with which justice-involved young people are often engaged.

In addition to the above reasons why a young person may choose to not disclose or discuss their ACEs is the simple fact that young people often are not able to see any link or connection between their ACEs and their offending behaviour. As a result, they do not see the relevance or value in talking about ACEs; which, as noted above, they would rather not do. On top of all of these barriers is the stark realization that many justice-involved young people are simply not aware that they have been exposed to any ACEs during their lives. For these young people, a childhood characterized by ACEs is sadly "just life":

YJW 8: I was trying to explain to this young lad that all this [his ACEs] was trauma [and] he was like "No, it's not. That's just life. Everybody has that."

DT 2: They don't think it is an adverse childhood experience. They just think it's their childhood experience and that's the norm.

YJW 5: Trauma is not a word that would come out of their mouth ... To them, it's their life, that's how it is.

Alongside these barriers is the time it takes to build a trusted relationship between a young person and their youth justice worker. For many years, research has highlighted the importance of building an effective working relationship when it comes to helping young people to desist from crime (Batchelor and McNeill 2005). Indeed, historically, the essence of much youth justice work was to 'provide a supportive relationship, based on the assumption that this relationship would be influential and would facilitate change' (Burnett 2004: 181). This is especially the case when it comes to discussing ACEs. As one of the workers noted, "if you're going to talk about trauma, ... you [need to] build a trusted relationship" (YJW 7). This view was supported by all of the workers who were interviewed:

YJW 10: Having those kind of conversations, those discussions [about ACEs], ... is about building up that relationship with them [the young person].

YJW 5: You have to build that trusting relationship before you start tapping into young people['s ACEs].

Nonetheless, all of the workers were also acutely aware that building a trusted relationship takes time and is not something that can be rushed; especially if the discussion is around ACEs:

YJW 1: Young people find the conversations [about ACEs] very difficult ... They need time to be able to trust the person they're talking to ... It could take a young person a long time to be able to trust their officer [enough] to have those actual conversations.

YJW 4: Not everyone is comfortable talking about it [ACEs], and that makes it difficult. It does take a long time.

The time required to build a sufficiently trusted relationship to start broaching the issue of ACEs is a key factor when it comes to the logistics of implementing trauma–informed practice. As shown below, while some of the workers felt that three months might be sufficient time for a young person to feel comfortable enough to disclose/discuss ACEs with their worker, others felt that you needed at least six months. This is particularly problematic if a young person is serving a short sentence:

YJW 8: A kid might have got a six-month order [but] it takes you three months to build that relationship.

YJW 4: I'd say most of your meaningful work doesn't get done until after six months' worth of trust ...

I mean, you can touch on stuff [earlier] but there is a point when you can tell that they trust you and they feel that they can speak [about ACEs].

YJW 1: Something like that [discussing ACEs] takes time. We might only be involved for six months and that kind of process, that journey that the young person needs to go through, sometimes takes longer than the time that you've actually got to work with that young person.

Notwithstanding the time it can take to build a trusted relationship, the development of a relationship where a young person trusts their youth justice worker enough to disclose or discuss their ACEs is key. As observed in Stubley and Young's (2022) work into complex trauma, it is only by developing a narrative about a traumatic event that a young person can begin to manage the impact of that event, and this can only begin with someone whom the young person trusts. Hopefully, the current move towards a Child First youth justice system (Youth Justice Board 2021) will help to give young people the space to work through some of their ACEs. As will be discussed in the following section, this does, however, raise the question whether or not youth justice workers have the necessary skills and available support to enable them to help young people unpack their trauma narratives. Additionally, there is the issue of vicarious trauma and the detrimental impact of this on workers who are expected to work in a trauma-informed way.

Before moving on to look this, it is important to highlight the external barriers (that is, those outside the youth justice service itself) that youth justice workers encounter when trying to deliver trauma-informed practice:

I: Are you aware of trauma-informed practice?
YJW 10: I think definitely in youth justice we are, and I think we have a good understanding of it and the impact it has on our young people. But I don't

> know whether outside of that [youth justice],
> whether they [other agencies] understand it.

While the youth justice service has arguably "got loads better at trauma-informed practice" (DT 2) over the last five years, all of the youth justice workers who were interviewed for this research felt that the same could not be said for the partner agencies that they work with. As one worker noted, "youth justice are trauma-informed, but court aren't [and] Police aren't" (YJW 8):

YJW 1: They [the courts] are coming round to it a little bit more, ... but it's definitely a work in progress. It [ACEs] is something that we're just introducing to the courts and getting them to think differently in terms of the way they're sentencing young people.

YJW 7: A police officer said to me [as] I was telling him about trauma, "if you're saying that he's suffered this, this and this" – he was talking about a particular kid who was really violent – "does that not make him more risky? He should go to prison." So it's about that lack of understanding.

If youth justice workers are frequently coming up against this "lack of understanding" of ACEs and the detrimental impact they can have on justice-involved young people, then this would indicate that some of the youth justice service's partner agencies require additional training around ACEs and trauma-informed practice. As neatly summarized by one worker:

YJW 8: We should all now be working from the same hymn book, ... have the same training, [and] be aware and understand ACEs ... If everybody was trauma-informed it would make everything a lot easier.

As recommended in the evaluation of the Enhanced Case Management project that was piloted in Wales, to ensure a consistent delivery of trauma-informed practice, all agencies dealing with young people who have a history of ACEs 'should consider training to improve their understanding of the impact of ACEs and trauma on the child's behaviour' (Glendinning et al 2021: 81). Indeed, as argued by SAMHSA (2014: 2), properly addressing ACEs and trauma requires a 'multi-pronged, multi-agency' approach.

Implementing a trauma-informed approach

It has been widely acknowledged that the delivery of trauma-informed practice within the justice system involves equipping youth justice workers with knowledge about ACEs and their effects, while also supporting them in their work with potentially traumatized young people (Liddle et al 2016). With this in mind, one of the aims of this research was to investigate whether youth justice workers need additional training and/or support to deliver trauma-informed practice to justice-involved young people. During their interviews, workers highlighted a range of training and support needs that they felt need to be addressed if they are to deliver effective trauma-informed practice. While workers acknowledged that they had received training on trauma-informed practice, thus giving them an awareness of the prevalence and effect of ACEs, what they felt was lacking was specific training in how to actually work through a young person's ACEs in a more therapeutic way:[3]

YJW 4: We've had a lot of training on it [trauma-informed practice], but I think what's missing is how we respond to that [ACEs] with the kids ... Because I'm always conscious that I'm going to say something that's going to trigger some kind of horrible memory for the young person and make them ... go home feeling worse than when they came in ... We're not trained therapists or anything like that.

YJW 1: Going into an interview with a young person that was just about to disclose to me an ACE, I could honestly say I wouldn't know where to start, ... because it isn't something that we've necessarily got expertise in.

It is clear that, despite having an awareness of ACEs and trauma-informed practice, feeling confident adopting a more therapeutic approach was an area in which many of the workers wanted additional training. Indeed, as evidenced in the quotes below, owing to the issues around trusted relationships outlined above, it would make sense to train youth justice workers to deliver more therapeutic work with those young people with whom they already have a trusted relationship. This was evidenced by one of the young people who was interviewed. When asked for his views on the drama therapist to whom he had been referred, he responded:

YP 1: I don't know him [and] I don't trust him. I won't say anything to him.

I: Do you think YOT staff would benefit from more therapeutic training?

YJW 2: Yes. Definitely ... Because so many [young] people will just not engage [with other workers] ... They don't want to talk to somebody [else], ... but they'll talk to us. But we haven't got the skills. That's not our area ... [But] if we all had this bag of skills, ... we could do more intensive work with people.

YJW 8: They've got Eclypse,[4] CAMHS,[5] drama therapy involved [but] a lot of my young people will turn around to me and say "I don't want to go to those individuals, but I'll come to you."

It is important to note, however, that this desire for more therapeutic training was not a view universally held among youth justice workers. For example, one worker felt that youth justice workers taking on multiple roles might be confusing for young people:

I: Do you think there's merit in giving staff therapeutic training?

YJW 6: Personally, no I don't ... I think it's about being really clear [to young people] about what your role is, and I think if you started training staff up to do counselling and [therapeutic] interventions it becomes quite confusing for a young person.

Notwithstanding this, the adoption of a therapeutic approach to support young people to acknowledge their emotional needs and talk about their ACEs has been identified as a key stage on the journey towards recovery (Bailey 1996; Levinson and Fonagy 2004). Accordingly, there has started to be a wider recognition of the need to develop a model of working that considers more therapeutic modalities. As Stubley (2022b: 38) notes, 'trauma-informed care requires a psychotherapeutic formulation that addresses the multiple ways in which trauma may have impacted upon that individual, and how best to offer interventions in response to this'. In line with this, since 2018 two drama therapists from the emotional trauma support team at One Education have been commissioned by the Manchester Youth Justice Service to deliver therapeutic interventions to justice-involved young people in the city.[6] As one of the therapists explained:

DT 2:   The case managers ... do their interviews and ... if there's significant trauma ... [or] if there's any ACEs, ... they tend to get referred to us straight away ... If the young person's willing to come and meet us, ... we'll arrange maybe five sessions to give it a try and see if they engage.

In their framework for working with traumatized young people, Lemma and Young (2022) advocate a minimum of six psychotherapeutically informed sessions to help orient a young person to the value of talking about the impact of any ACEs and trauma they may have experienced. The six sessions enable the processing of the traumatic event to begin, and the impact of the trauma to carefully unfold. By allowing a young person to start making sense of their traumatic experience in a way that is 'containing', the risk of them 'acting out in destructive ways' is reduced (Lemma and Young 2022: 105).

The youth justice workers were particularly appreciative of the drama therapists. As one of them noted, "I think they're amazing at what they do ... I do feel that we don't have them enough in our service" (YJW 8). As mentioned above, the youth justice workers were mindful that working in a trauma-informed way increases the likelihood that they might unwittingly "trigger some kind of horrible memory for the young person and make them ... go home feeling worse than when they came in" (YJW 4). However, having skilled therapists on hand to work through young people's ACEs in a clinical way, as opposed to expecting youth justice workers to do this, means that the chances of workers unintentionally triggering any negative emotions when discussing ACEs – emotions that they may not have the skills to properly resolve – are reduced. As one of the workers noted:

YJW 5: It can't be the YOS [Youth Offending Service] opening a can of worms and then letting that young person leave. Maybe it could be all these [young] people see a therapist ... to talk about those ACEs and then they [the therapist can] close that door so the young person can leave in a good space and hit the streets in a good place. Rather than them going out really upset and doing something stupid because they don't understand the emotions that they're going through.

While the two drama therapists have been commissioned to deliver a service to young people with ACEs, the fact remains that some workers find working in a trauma–informed way "emotionally hard". Yet, if the expectation is that youth justice workers are to deliver trauma-informed practice, it is clear that they should be 'assisted in building their own psychological resilience – mapping out their own vulnerabilities and strengths and protecting themselves against vicarious trauma' (Liddle et al 2016: 52). They should also be able to 'disclose and explore their emotions in a supportive environment in order to manage their feelings effectively' (Liddle et al 2016: 52).

YJW 6: It's emotionally hard. When I think about some of my cases, I've gone home and cried because it's just so distressing, and you've got to be able to process that yourself, haven't you and my God that's hard … [Yet] we're putting people in this position and giving them no outlet.

To directly address this issue, the two drama therapists were also commissioned to provide clinical supervision to any worker who felt they needed it:

DT 2: Because they're working in a more trauma–informed way, … they're carrying a lot more, … [and] so they need that emotional help to look after themselves, to keep up that self-care.

While some of the workers felt that clinical supervision should be integral to any training around trauma-informed practice, others felt that clinical supervision should just be available as and when a worker may need it:

YJW 6: I think any form of [trauma-informed practice] training needs to come along with … good-quality clinical supervision for the staff too, to think about

how they process and think about the hideous
trauma stories that they're hearing.

YJW 2: I got allocated a case a while back and ... it was
just overwhelming, ... really heavy ... So I spoke
to management ... and I've been offered ... sessions
with the drama therapist as a debrief so that I can
kind of get rid of it. And I think it's needed,
because it's hard, hard stuff.

Being affected by vicarious trauma as a result of processing
young people's trauma narratives can be an extremely
challenging experience, especially for untrained youth justice
workers. As recognized in wider therapeutic literature, the need
for traumatized young people to feel powerful and in control,
while denying any feelings of vulnerability and dependency,
is especially acute following a traumatic experience (Lemma
and Young 2022). This was evident in the previously discussed
quote: "I think they'd rather be angry and shouting and have
that confrontation, than feel exposed and vulnerable" (DT 2).
For some workers, this combination of bearing witness to
tragic life histories with the responsibility to 'contain' (Bion
1963) traumatic stories can be overwhelming. Accordingly,
to ensure the psychological safety of both young people and
their workers, it is imperative that clinical therapeutic support
is made available to those tasked with working in a trauma-
informed way.

EIGHT

Conclusions

Recommendations

Based on the findings described in the preceding chapters, this research makes the following recommendations:

- *Deliver training around implementing trauma-informed practice*
  While youth justice workers acknowledged that they had received some general training on adverse childhood experiences (ACEs) and trauma informed approaches, what they felt was lacking was more specific training in how to implement trauma-informed practice in a more psychotherapeutic way. Training to address this need should be delivered by qualified professionals.
- *Deliver training across the wider youth justice system*
  Funding should be made available for qualified professionals to deliver training on ACEs and trauma-informed practice to other bodies in the youth justice system, such as the courts, the police and the secure estate. This will help to embed an awareness of ACEs and trauma-informed practice throughout the justice system. This systemic approach is necessary to ensure that young people receive a consistent, trauma-informed service, irrespective of which stage of the system they are at.
- *Provide psychotherapeutic support to those young people who need it*
  Clinical psychotherapeutic support around trauma should be readily available to those young people who may need it (see Lemma and Young 2022). The responsibility for delivering this particular support should not lie with youth

justice workers. Placing it with them has the potential to harm both youth justice workers and young people. Instead, as is the case in Manchester, clinical support should be delivered by qualified professionals based within youth justice services.

- *Offer clinical supervision to youth justice workers*
  If youth justice workers are expected to deliver trauma-informed practice, then the opportunity for clinical supervision with a qualified professional should be made available to protect them from vicarious trauma. This provision should be in addition to any other supervision procedures that youth justice services currently offer.

- *Support young people to meaningfully participate*
  In line with a Child First approach (Youth Justice Board 2021), justice-involved young people should be supported and encouraged to participate in the development of trauma-informed responses to serious youth violence (SYV) as they are 'by far the most beneficial group to involve' (Fraser and Irwin-Rogers 2021: 17). Encouraging and supporting young people to tell their stories and describe their experiences and opinions provides an opportunity for professionals to create more individualized responses to SYV (Smithson et al 2021).

- *Avoid quantifying ACEs as a measure of risk*
  Simply quantifying ACEs and interpreting them as a measure of the risk of becoming involved in SYV (either as perpetrator or victim) is at odds with trauma-informed approaches to working with justice-involved young people. Instead, the advancement of high-quality, trauma-informed policy and practice should rely on the identification of ACEs and an understanding of the impact ACEs might have on individual young people. Considering the impact of psychosocial factors, this knowledge and understanding should then be used to develop individualized approaches to addressing young people's involvement in SYV.

Rethinking the future of trauma-informed practice with justice-involved young people

Recent literature from those working specifically in the field of trauma emphasizes the importance of developing a framework for intervening with young people who have experienced ACEs (for a further discussion see Lemma and Young 2022). This psychotherapeutic way of working helps unpack the trauma by discussing the ways in which ACEs can impact a young person's ability to manage and regulate their emotions and impulses. It is well recognized within this field that individuals will vary in their responses to ACEs, and each individual will attach a specific personal meaning to their experience(s) which will be reflected in the ways in which they engage with society at large.

This personal meaning is specific to that individual, and not dissimilar to a bicycle lock with a four-number combination (Yakeley and Adshead 2013). The first two numbers of the lock are static (for example, being young and male) while the third is dynamic (for example, substance use or mental health issues).[1] The fourth number is the individual's state of mind at the time of the offence. This fourth number, when combined with the other three, can either assist or inhibit the mechanisms that prevent violent behaviour. As Gilligan (2003) notes, violence is often precipitated by experiences that cause feelings of shame and humiliation. In these instances, unbearable and overwhelming traumatic childhood memories can be triggered that can exacerbate these feelings to the point where they overwhelm the affect regulation system of the perpetrator, resulting in violence. It is important to note that not every individual with three risky numbers on the bicycle lock will become violent, as many young people who have been exposed to ACEs never go on to perpetrate SYV. Nonetheless, understanding that some young people have the potential to engage in SYV, and the mechanisms through which this might occur, is crucial if we are to work in a trauma-informed way that takes seriously the theoretical underpinnings of forensic psychotherapy (Gilligan 2019).

There are currently promising models of trauma-informed practice evident in the youth justice secure estate that are working in a psychotherapeutically informed way (Taylor et al 2018; Anna Freud Centre 2022). These models have illuminated that, when working with young people who have experienced ACEs, a trained workforce, underpinned with clinical support to enable all of those involved to comprehend the extent of the trauma, is essential. It is only with a trained workforce in place, combined with a radical shift towards quality-assured, trauma-informed practice, that we can begin to address the potential relationship between ACES and a young person's violent offending behaviour. Moreover, the need to support youth justice workers with clinical supervision where appropriate should be regarded as a priority. The young people involved in this research clearly stated their preparedness to discuss their ACEs only with a trusted adult, who in most cases was their youth justice worker.

Despite the obvious need for robust, trauma-informed practice, when it comes to embedding this in organizational cultures there still remains a lack of understanding and appetite among wider youth justice agencies. This is understandable, owing to the historic view that the youth justice system is a place of punishment and retribution, not of safety and support. This is in direct contradiction to the ideologies of Child First (Youth Justice Board 2021) and Participatory Youth Practice (PYP) (Smithson et al 2021). We need to drastically rethink our offer of support for justice-involved young people if we are to break the link between ACEs and serious violence. Accordingly, it is a matter of utmost priority that we move towards more clinically informed therapeutic practices. Not only will such a shift enable youth justice agencies to address SYV more effectively, but it will also help to develop a more humane approach to vulnerable young people who find themselves adrift in a sea of justice agencies with nothing to cling to.

Limitations

While this research has contributed to the evidence base for the relationship between ACEs and SYV, and the importance of trauma-informed practice with justice-involved young people, the research team recognize and acknowledge that the research did have a number of limitations.

Firstly, the young people involved in the research were all teenage men. This reflects the fact that only a small number of young women perpetrate SYV offences in Manchester. The research team do, however, recognize that women can be affected by SYV in other ways (Horan et al 2019; Jump and Horan 2021). Furthermore, as noted in the Youth Violence Commission's final report (Irwin Rogers et al 2020), women, including family members and friends, very often provide protective and nurturing roles to young men involved with SYV but are rarely given the space to grieve and heal. The report highlights the need for funding in this area to ensure that women who have experienced violence, either physically or vicariously, receive the support and therapy they require. It is clear that further research that focusses specifically on the gendered relationship between ACEs and SYV is needed.

Second is the issue of race. The Black Lives Matter movement and the protests held over the summer of 2020 led to a focus on the issue of structural and systemic racism. For instance, Black, Asian and minority ethnic (BAME) young people are more than twice as likely to live in poverty as those from white families (Lammy Review 2017). Research has found that school exclusion rates for black Caribbean students in English schools are up to six times higher than those of their white peers in some local authorities (Perera 2020). This is particularly worrying when one considers the clear relationship between exclusions and involvement in SYV as a perpetrator and/or a victim (Irwin-Rogers and Harding 2018). In a youth justice context, the disproportional numbers of BAME young people in the system remains pronounced. For example, stop-and-search rates in BAME communities remain depressingly high when compared with white communities, and BAME young people make up half of all young people in custody (Lammy Review 2017). It has been argued that the Police, Crime, Sentencing and Courts Act 2022 will further increase racial disparity in the youth justice system as it fails to introduce measures to effectively address child criminal exploitation and violence, which disproportionately impacts BAME young people (Alliance for Youth Justice 2021). There is clearly much more work to be done to address racism and its impact on justice-involved young people. In any future debate or discussion about SYV and how to respond to it, there must be a focus on race.

Traumatic events do not discriminate and will arguably converge around gender, ethnicity, age, class and sexuality. All of these intersecting factors will influence how a traumatic event is experienced and worked through, and therefore one must also consider how young people's lives are shaped by the broader church of social and cultural relationships.

Notes

one Introduction

[1] The Index of Multiple Deprivation is used within the UK to classify the relative deprivation of small areas. Multiple components of deprivation are weighted with different strengths and compiled into a single score.

[2] The gravity score describes an offence's seriousness with scores ranging from one (least serious) through to eight (most serious).

[3] Per 10,000 persons aged 10–17-years in the general population.

[4] The Youth Justice Board is an executive, non-departmental, public body sponsored by the Ministry of Justice, responsible for overseeing the youth justice system in England and Wales. The Board took the rate of SYV offences for each of the 157 youth justice services in England and Wales and identified those services that had been in the top quartile for three or more quarters during the 2017/18 financial year. From that group, the Board assigned 12 youth justice services to be part of a SYV Reference Group and to receive funding as pathfinders.

[5] The *Manchester Evening News* is a regional daily newspaper that covers Manchester.

[6] The Crime Survey for England and Wales has measured crime since 1981. Used alongside police recorded crime data it is a valuable source of information for the government about the extent and nature of crime in England and Wales.

[7] The Youth Endowment Fund (YEF) was established in March 2019 with a £200 million endowment and a ten-year mandate from the Home Office. The YEF aims to prevent young people aged 10–14 from getting caught up in crime and violence by making sure that those at most risk get the best possible support.

[8] While Knife Crime Prevention Orders can be issued to a young person who has been convicted of a relevant offence, they can also be issued to a person who is simply considered to be at risk of becoming involved in knife crime.

[9] www.mmu.ac.uk/mcys/

two Review of the Literature

[1] The Youth Endowment Fund (YEF) was established in March 2019 by children's charity Impetus, with a £200 million endowment and a ten-year mandate from the Home Office.

[2] Serious Violence Reduction Orders can be given to a person who has been convicted of offences where a knife or offensive weapon was used or was present. The police will have powers to stop and search those given the orders.

[3] In England and Wales, Youth Offending Teams are multi-agency partnerships that deliver youth justice services locally (see www.gov.uk/youth-offending-team).

[4] The secure estate for young people in England and Wales includes young offender institutions, secure training centres and secure children's homes.

[5] Secure children's homes accommodate vulnerable young people, typically aged 10 to 17, in small establishments with high staff-to-child ratios.

[6] If a young person is considered to be suffering or likely to suffer significant harm, the local authority will make them the subject of a child protection plan (in England) or add them to a child protection register (in Northern Ireland, Scotland and Wales).

[7] Section 53 of the Children and Young Persons Act 1933 was introduced to make special provision for the custody of young people under the age of 18 years who were convicted by the Crown Court for murder and other grave (primarily violent) crimes. Section 53 was repealed in August 2000 and its provisions were transferred to Sections 90, 91 and 92 of the Powers of Criminal Courts (Sentencing) Act 2000.

[8] In this study, self-directed violence included self-harm, suicidal ideation and attempted suicide.

[9] In the US study of 11–20-year-old male and female offenders in custody, by Hux et al (1998), TBI was defined as 'head injury resulting in concussion'. In the UK study of 16–18-year-old male offenders in custody, by Davies et al (2012), TBI was defined as 'any head injury resulting in loss of consciousness or feeling dazed and confused'. Both studies summarized in Hughes et al 2015b.

three Researching Adverse Childhood Experiences and Trauma

[1] IBM-SPSS Statistics is a software package for performing quantitative data analysis.

[2] See www.oneeducation.co.uk

[3] NVivo is a software package for performing qualitative data analysis.

[4] A Section 18 assault is known as grievous bodily harm, and is detailed in Section 18 of the Offences Against the Person Act 1861. The offence must include wounding with intent or with intent to cause grievous bodily harm. In UK law, a Section 18 assault is the most serious form of violence that can be committed (short of murder or manslaughter).

This offence is indictable only, which means it can only be dealt with in the Crown Court. The maximum sentence is life imprisonment.

5 An ACEs assessment was not completed for this young person.
6 See www.mmu.ac.uk/mcys/current-research--activities/kicking-crime-into-touch/
7 AQA's Unit Award Scheme is used to record learner achievement. It builds confidence and acts as a stepping-stone towards further education, employment and training – see https://www.aqa.org.uk/programmes/unit-award-scheme
8 See https://vimeo.com/551504469
9 See https://stummuac.sharepoint.com/sites/aca-ah-mcys/Shared%20Documents/Forms/AllItems.aspx?id=%2Fsites%2Faca%2Dah%2Dmcys%2FShared%20Documents%2FSYV%2FTrauma%20City%20%2D%20A%20Tale%20of%20SYV%2Ep dfand parent=%2Fsites%2Faca%2Dah%2Dmcys%2FShared%20Documents%2FSYV

four Serious Youth Violence

1 Proven offences are those for which a youth caution or sentence was received.
2 The other youth justice services in the Youth Justice Board's Reference Group included Brent, Croydon, Greenwich, Haringey, Islington, Lambeth, Lewisham, Luton, Nottingham, Sandwell and Southampton.
3 These are young people (aged 10–17), resident in England and Wales, who have received their first reprimand, warning, caution or conviction for a recordable offence.
4 As measured using the three Manchester Youth Justice Teams: North, Central, and South.

seven Trauma-informed Practice

1 Youth Offending Team.
2 The six key principles are safety; trustworthiness and transparency; peer support; collaboration and mutuality; empowerment, voice and choice; and addressing cultural, historical and gender issues.
3 It will be interesting to see whether the Youth Justice Board's Effective Practice Award in 'trauma-informed practice' (launched in spring 2020) addresses this training need.
4 Eclypse helps young people in Manchester who want advice and support about their own or somebody else's drug or alcohol use.

5   CAMHS (which stands for Child and Adolescent Mental Health Services) provide services that assess and treat young people with emotional, behavioural or mental health difficulties.

6   The therapists are mindful that the term 'drama therapy' might discourage justice-involved young people from engaging with the service. As such, when they are initially explaining the service to those young people referred to them, they tend to use the more generic term 'creative therapy'.

eight Conclusions

1   Static factors are unchangeable, while dynamic factors have the potential to change over time.

References

Alliance for Youth Justice (2021) *AYJ Response: Police, Crime, Sentencing and Courts Bill – Implications for Children and the Youth Justice System*, www.ayj.org.uk/news-content/pcsc-bill-response

American Psychiatric Association (2013) *Diagnostic and Statistical Manual of Mental Disorders* (5th edition), Washington: American Psychiatric Association.

Anda, R.F., Felitti, V.J., Bremner, J.D., Walker, J.D., Whitfield, C. and Perry, B.D., et al (2006) 'The enduring effects of abuse and related adverse experiences in childhood. A convergence of evidence from neurobiology and epidemiology', *European Archives of Psychiatry and Clinical Neuroscience*, 256(3):174–186.

Anderson, S.L., Tomada, A., Vincow, E.S., Valente, E., Polcari, A. and Teicher, M.H. (2008) 'Preliminary evidence for sensitive periods in the effect of childhood sexual abuse on regional brain development', *Journal of Neuropsychiatry and Clinical Neurosciences*, 20(3):292–301.

Anna Freud Centre (2022) *Independent Evaluation of the Framework for Integrated Care (SECURE STAIRS)*, London: Anna Freud National Centre for Children and Families.

Asmussen, K., Fischer, F., Drayton, E. and McBride, T. (2020) *Adverse Childhood Experiences: What We Know, What We Don't Know, and What Should Happen Next*, London: Early Intervention Foundation.

Avison Young (2022) *Economic and Property Market Review March 2022*, Manchester: Avison Young.

Baglivio, M.T., Epps, N., Swart, K., Huq, M.S., Sheer, A. and Hardt, N.S. (2014) 'The prevalence of Adverse Childhood Experiences (ACE) in the lives of juvenile offenders', *Journal of Juvenile Justice*, 3(2):1–17.

Baglivio, M.T., Wolff, K.T. and Epps, N. (2021) 'Violent juveniles' adverse childhood experiences: differentiating victim groups', *Journal of Criminal Justice*, 72(2001):101769.

Bailey, S. (1996) 'Psychiatric assessment of the violent child and adolescent: towards understanding and safe intervention', in V. Varma (ed) *Violence in Children and Adolescents*, London: Jessica Kingsley.

Baker, K. (2012) *AssetPlus Rationale*, London: Youth Justice Board.

Batchelor, S. and McNeill, F. (2005) 'The young person–worker relationship', in T. Bateman and J. Pitts (eds) *The RHP Companion to Youth Justice*, Lyme Regis: Russell House Publishing.

Bath, H.I. (2008) 'Calming together: the pathway to self-control', *Reclaiming Children and Youth*, 16(4):44–46.

Bauer, J.J. and McAdams, D.P. (2004) 'Personal growth in adults' stories of life transitions', *Journal of Personality*, 72:573–602.

Baumeister, R.F. and Leary, M.R. (1995) 'The need to belong: desire for interpersonal attachments as a fundamental human motivation', *Psychological Bulletin*, 117(3):497–529.

Beckett, K., Farr, M., Kothari, A., Wye, L. and le May, A. (2018) 'Embracing complexity and uncertainty to create impact: exploring the processes and transformative potential of co-produced research through development of a social impact model', *Health Research Policy and Systems*, 16:118.

Billingham, L. and Irwin-Rogers, K. (2022) *Against Youth Violence: A Social Harm Perspective*, Bristol: Bristol University Press.

Bion, W.R. (1963) *Elements of Psycho-Analysis*, London: Karnac Books.

Boswell, G. (1996) *Young and Dangerous: The Backgrounds and Careers of Section 53 offenders*, Aldershot: Ashgate.

Bowlby, J. (1944) 'Forty-four juvenile thieves: their characters and home-life', *The International Journal of Psycho-analysis*, 25(19).

Bowlby, J. (1950) 'Research into the origins of delinquent behaviour', *British Medical Journal,* 1(4653): 570–573.

Bowlby, J. (1969) *Attachment and Loss*, New York: Basic Books.

Bowlby, J. (1980) *Loss, Sadness and Depression*, New York: Basic Books.

Bowlby, J. (1988) *A Secure Base: Clinical Applications of Attachment Theory*, London: Routledge.

Braga, T., Goncalves, L.C., Basto-Perpeira, M. and Maia, A. (2017) 'Unraveling the link between maltreatment and juvenile antisocial behavior: a meta-analysis of prospective longitudinal studies', *Aggression and Violent Behavior*, 33:37–50.

Braun, V. and Clarke, V. (2006) 'Using thematic analysis in psychology', *Qualitative Research in Psychology*, 3(2):77–101.

Brennan, I.R. and Moore, S.C. (2009) 'Weapons and violence: a review of theory and research', *Aggression and Violent Behavior*, 14(3):215–225.

Brooks, J. and King, N. (2014) *Doing Template Analysis; Evaluating an End-of-Life Care Service*, London: SAGE Publications.

Burnett, R. (2004) 'One-to-one ways of promoting desistance: in search of an evidence base', in R. Burnett and C. Roberts (eds) *What Works in Probation and Youth Justice: Developing Evidence-Based Practice*, Cullompton: Willan.

Byrne, B. and Lundy, L. (2019) 'Children's rights-based childhood policy: a six-P framework', *The International Journal of Human Rights*, 23(3):357–373.

Case, S.P. and Haines, K.R. (2015) 'Children first, offenders second positive promotion: re-framing the prevention debate', *Youth Justice*, 15(3):226–239.

Catalani, C. and Minkler, M. (2010) 'Photovoice: A review of the literature in health and public health', *Health Education and Behavior*, 37(3):424–451.

Centers for Disease Control and Prevention (n.d.) *Adverse Childhood Experiences (ACEs)*, www.cdc.gov/violenceprevention/aces/

Centers for Disease Control and Prevention (2021) *Adverse Childhood Experiences Prevention Strategy*, Atlanta, GA: National Center for Injury Prevention and Control, Centers for Disease Control and Prevention, www.cdc.gov/injury/pdfs/priority/ACEs-Strategic-Plan_Final_508.pdf

Chase, S.E. (2005) 'Narrative inquiry: multiple lenses, approaches, voices', in N.K. Denzin and Y.S. Lincoln (eds) *The Sage Handbook of Qualitative Research*, Thousand Oaks, CA: Sage Publications, Inc.

Cleaton, M.A.M. and Kirby, A. (2018) 'Why do we find it so hard to calculate the burden of neurodevelopmental disorders?', *Journal of Child Developmental Disorders*, 4:10.

Cordis Bright (2017) *Evaluation of the Enhanced Case Management Approach*, Social Research Number 16/2007, Cardiff: Welsh Government.

Craig, J.M., Piquero, A.R., Farrington, D.P. and Ttofi, M.M. (2017a) 'A little early risk goes a long bad way: adverse childhood experiences and life-course offending in the Cambridge study', *Journal of Criminal Justice*, 53(2017):34–45.

Craig, J.M., Baglivio, M.T., Wolff, K.T., Piquero, A.R. and Epps, N. (2017b) 'Do social bonds buffer the impact of adverse childhood experiences on reoffending?', *Youth Violence and Juvenile Justice*, 15(1):3–20.

Criminal Justice Joint Inspection (2021) *Neurodiversity in the Criminal Justice System: A Review of Evidence*, London: HM Inspectorate of Prisons and HM Inspectorate of Probation.

Curran, L. (2013) *101 Trauma-Informed Interventions: Activities, Exercises and Assignments to Move the Client and Therapy Forward*, Wisconsin: PESI Publishing.

Dahlberg, L.L. and Krug, E.G. (2002) 'Violence – a global public health problem', in E.G. Krug, L.L. Dahlberg, J.A. Mercy, A.B. Zwi and R. Lozano (eds) *World Report on Violence and Health*, Geneva: World Health Organization.

Dempsey, M. (2021) *Still Not Safe: The Public Health Response to Youth Violence*, London: Children's Commissioner for England.

Densley, J. (2020) 'Collective violence online: when street gangs use social media', in C.A. Ireland, M. Lewis, A.C. Lopez and J.L. Ireland (eds) *The Handbook of Collective Violence: Current Developments and Understanding*, Abingdon: Routledge.

Dent-Brown, K. and Wang, M. (2006) 'The mechanism of story-making: a grounded theory study of the 6-part story method', *The Arts in Psychotherapy*, 33:316–330.

De Zulueta, F. (2006) *From Pain to Violence: The Traumatic Roots of Destructiveness*, New York: Wiley.

Dierkhising, C., Ko, S., Woods-Jaeger, B., Briggs, E., Lee, R. and Pynoos, R. (2013) 'Trauma histories among justice-involved youth: findings from the National Child Traumatic Stress Network', *European Journal of Psychotraumatology,* 2013(4):20274.

Dinkler, L., Lundström, S., Gajwani, R., Lichtenstein, P., Gillberg, C. and Minnis, H. (2017) 'Maltreatment-associated neurodevelopmental disorders: a co-twin control analysis', *Journal of Child Psychology and Psychiatry*, 58(6):691–701.

Duke, N.N., Pettingell, S.L., McMorris, B.J. and Borowsky, I.W. (2010) 'Adolescent violence perpetration: associations with multiple types of adverse childhood experiences', *Pediatrics*, 125(4):778–786.

Dwivedi, K.N. (1997) *The Therapeutic Use of Story*, London: Routledge.

Elliott, G., Kao, S. and Grant, A-M. (2004) 'Mattering: empirical validation of a social-psychological concept', *Self and Identity*, 3(4):339–354.

Farrington, D.P. (1997) 'Early prediction of violent and nonviolent youthful offending', *European Journal on Criminal Policy and Research*, 5:51–66.

Felitti, V.J., Anda, R.F., Nordenberg, D., Williamson, D.F., Spitz, A.M., Edwards, V. and Marks, J.S. (1998) 'Relationship of childhood abuse and household dysfunction to many of the leading causes of death in adults: the Adverse Childhood Experiences (ACE) study', *American Journal of Preventative Medicine*, 14(4):245–258.

Firmin, C.E. and Knowles, R. (2020) *The Legal and Policy Framework for Contextual Safeguarding Approaches. A 2020 Update on the 2018 legal briefing*, Contextual Safeguarding Network.

Fivush, R. and Merrill, N. (2016) 'An ecological systems approach to family narratives', *Memory Studies,* 9:305–14.

Flett, G. (2018) *The Psychology of Mattering: Understanding the Human Need to be Significant*, London: Academic Press.

Fonagy, P. and Target, M. (1995) 'Understanding the violent patient: the use of the body and the role of the father', *International Journal of Psycho-Analysis*, 76:487–501.

Fonagy, P. and Target, M. (1996) 'Playing with reality: I. Theory of mind and the normal development of psychic reality', *International Journal of Psychoanalysis*, 77(2):217–233.

Fonagy, P., Target, M., Steele, M., Steele, H., Leigh, T., Levinson, A. and Kennedy, R. (1997) 'Morality, disruptive behavior, borderline personality disorder, crime and their relationship to security of attachment', in L. Atkinson and K.J. Zucker (eds) *Attachment and Psychopathology*, New York: Guilford Press.

Foster-Fishman, P., Nowell, B., Deacon, Z., Nievar, M.A. and McCann, P. (2005) 'Using methods that matter: the impact of reflection, dialogue, and voice', *American Journal of Community Psychology*, 36:275–291.

Fox, B., Perez, N., Cass, E., Baglivio, M. and Epps, N. (2015) 'Trauma changes everything: examining the relationship between adverse childhood experiences and serious, violent and chronic juvenile offenders', *Child Abuse and Neglect*, 46:163–173.

Fraser, A. and Irwin-Rogers, K. (2021) A *Public Health Approach to Violence Reduction: Strategic Briefing*, Dartington: Research in Practice.

Freud, S. (1916) *Introductory Lectures on Psychoanalysis,* SE 15–6:13–477.

Freud, S. (1920) 'Beyond the pleasure principle', in S. Freud (1955) *The Standard Edition of the Complete Psychological Works of Sigmund Freud, Volume XVIII (1920–1922)*, London: The Hogarth Press.

Frey, W. (2018) 'Humanizing digital mental health through social media: centering experiences of gang-involved youth exposed to high rates of violence', *Biomedical Informatics Insights*, 10:1–5.

Garland, C. (1998) *Understanding Trauma. A Psychoanalytical Approach*, London: Duckworth.

Gersie, A. (1992) *Earthtales: Storytelling in Times of Change*, London: Green Print.

Gilligan, J. (1996) *Violence: Our Deadly Epidemic and its Causes*, New York: G.P. Putnam.

Gilligan, J. (2003) 'Shame, guilt and violence', *Social Research,* 70(4):1149–1180.

Gilligan, J. (2019) 'What is forensic psychotherapy? Reflections on a new discipline', *International Journal of Forensic Psychotherapy*, 1(1):1–9.

Glendinning, F., Rodriguez, G.R., Newbury, A. and Wilmott, R. (2021) *Adverse Childhood Experience (ACE) and Trauma-Informed Approaches in Youth Justice Services in Wales: An Evaluation of the Implementation of the Enhanced Case Management (ECM) project*, Wales: Bangor University.

Goff, A., Rose, E., Rose, S. and Purves, D. (2007) 'Does PTSD occur in sentenced prison populations? A systematic literature review', *Criminal Behaviour and Mental Health*, 17:152–162.

Gray, P. (2008) 'Misunderstood Youth? A Psychosocial Study of Young Men Leaving Custody', PhD thesis, Keele: Keele University.

Gray, P. (2010) 'The resettlement needs of young offenders leaving custody: an emotional dimension', *Prison Service Journal*, 189:25–28.

Gray, P. (2015) '"I hate talking about it": identifying and supporting traumatised young people in custody', *The Howard Journal*, 54(5):434–450.

Greater Manchester Poverty Action (2022) *Greater Manchester Poverty Monitor 2022*, www.gmpovertyaction.org/poverty-moni tor-2022/

Habermas, T. and Silveira, C. (2008) 'The development of global coherence in life narratives across adolescence: temporal, causal, and thematic aspects', *Developmental Psychology,* 44(3):707–721.

Haines, K. and Case, S. (2015) *Positive Youth Justice: Children First, Offenders Second*, London: Policy Press.

Hawkins, J.D., Herrenkohl, T.I., Farrington, D.P., Brewer, D., Catalano, R.F., Harachi, T.W. and Cothern, L. (2000) 'Predictors of youth violence', *Office of Juvenile Justice and Delinquency Prevention Juvenile Justice Bulletin*, April 2000.

Her Majesty's Inspectorate of Probation (2017) *The Work of Youth Offending Teams to Protect the Public*, Manchester: HM Inspectorate of Probation.

Herman, J.L. (2015) *Trauma and Recovery: The Aftermath of Violence – from Domestic Abuse to Political Terror*, New York: Basic Books.

Hinshelwood, R. (1989) *A Dictionary of Kleinian Thought*, London: Free Association Press.

Home Office (2018) *Serious Violence Strategy*, London: HM Government.

Home Office (2020) *Violence Reduction Unit Interim Guidance*, London: Home Office.

Home Office (2021) 'Knife Crime Prevention Orders begin in London', www.gov.uk/government/news/knife-crime-prevent ion-orders-begin-in-london

Home Office (2022) 'Serious Violence Reduction Orders: Police, Crime, Sentencing and Courts Act 2022', www.gov.uk/governm ent/publications/police-crime-sentencing-and-courts-bill-2021- factsheets/police-crime-sentencing-and-courts-bill-2021-seri ous-violence-reduction-orders-factsheet

Horan, R., Jump, D. and O'Shea, S. (2019) *Phase One Process Evaluation Report: The Getting Out For Good (GOFG) Project*, Warrington: The Averment Group.

Hudson-Sharp, N. and Runge, J. (2017*) International Trends in Insecure Work: A Report for the Trades Union Congress*, London: National Institute of Economic and Social Research.

Hughes, K., Hardcastle, K. and Perkins, C. (2015a) *The Mental Health Needs of Gang-affiliated Young People*, London: Public Health England.

Hughes, N., Williams, W.H., Chitsabesan, P., Walesby, R.C., Mounce, L.T.A. and Clasby, B. (2015b) 'The prevalence of traumatic brain injury among young offenders in custody', *Journal of Head Trauma Rehabilitation,* 30(2):94–105.

Irwin-Rogers, K. (2019) 'Illicit drug markets, consumer capitalism and the rise of social media: a toxic trap for young people', *Critical Criminology,* 27(4):591–610.

Irwin-Rogers, K. and Harding, S. (2018) 'Challenging the orthodoxy on pupil gang involvement: when two social fields collide', *British Educational Research Journal*, 44(3):463–479.

Irwin-Rogers, K. and Pinkney, C. (2017) *Social Media as a Catalyst and Trigger for Youth Violence*, London: Catch22.

Irwin-Rogers, K., Densley, J. and Pinkney, C. (2018) 'Social media and gang violence', in J.L. Ireland, P. Birch and C.A. Ireland (eds) *International Handbook on Aggression*, Abingdon: Routledge.

Irwin-Rogers, K., Muthoo, A. and Billingham, L. (2020) *Youth Violence Commission Final Report*.

Jacobson, J., Bhardwa, B., Gyateng, T., Hunter, G. and Hough, M. (2010) *Punishing Disadvantage: A Profile of Children in Custody*, London: Prison Reform Trust.

Jahanshahi, B., Murray, K. and McVie, S. (2022) 'ACEs, places and inequality: understanding the effects of adverse childhood experiences and poverty on offending in childhood', *The British Journal of Criminology*, 62(3):751–772.

Joliffe, D., Farrington, D.P., Loeber, R. and Pardini, D. (2016) 'Protective factors for violence: results from the Pittsburgh Youth Study', *Journal of Criminal Justice*, 45:32–40.

Jump, D. (2014) 'Fighting for Change: Narrative accounts on the appeal and desistance potential of boxing', PhD thesis, Manchester: University of Manchester.

Jump, D. (2020) *The Criminology of Boxing, Violence and Desistance*, Bristol: Bristol University Press.

Jump, D. and Horan, R. (2021) *Getting Out for Good: Preventing Gangs through Participation*, Academic Insights 2021/12, Manchester: HM Inspectorate of Probation.

Jump, D. and Smithson, H. (2020) 'Dropping your guard: the use of boxing as a means of forming desistance narratives amongst young people in the criminal justice system', *The International Journal of Sport and Society*, 11(2):56–69.

Kirby, A. (2021) *Neurodiversity – A Ehole-Child Approach for Youth Justice*, Academic Insights 2021/08, Manchester: HM Inspectorate of Probation.

Kirby, A., Clasby, B., Williams, H. and Megan-Cleaton, M. (2020) 'Young men in prison with neurodevelopmental disorders: missed, misdiagnosed and misinterpreted', *Prison Service Journal*, 251:46–58.

Lammy Review (2017) *An independent review into the treatment of, and outcomes for, Black, Asian and Minority Ethnic individuals in the Criminal Justice System*, https://assets.publishing.service.gov.uk/government/uploads/system/uploads/attachment_data/file/643001/lammy-review-final-report.pdf

Langhinrichsen-Rohling, J., Arata, C., O'Brien, N., Bowers, D. and Klibert, J. (2006) 'Sensitive research with adolescents: just how upsetting are self-report surveys anyway?', *Violence and Victims*, 21(4):425–444.

Lemma, A. and Young, L. (2022) 'Working with traumatized adolescents: a framework for intervention', in J. Stubley and L. Young (eds) *Complex Trauma. The Tavistock Model*, Abingdon: Routledge.

Levinson, A. and Fonagy, P. (2004) 'Offending and attachment: the relationship between interpersonal awareness and offending in a prison population with psychiatric disorder', *Canadian Journal of Psychoanalysis*, 12(2):225–251.

Liddle, M., Boswell, G., Wright, S. and Francis, V. (2016) *Trauma and Young Offenders: A review of the research and practice literature*, London: Beyond Youth Custody.

Lubit, R., Rovine, D., Defrancisci, L. and Eth, S. (2003) 'Impact of trauma on children', *Journal of Psychiatric Practice*, 9(2):128–138.

Maas, C., Herrenkohl, T. and Sousa, C. (2008) 'Review of research on child maltreatment and violence in youth', *Trauma, Violence and Abuse*, 9(1):56–67.

Martin, A., Nixon, C., Watt, C.L., Taylor, A. and Kennedy, P. (2021) 'Exploring the prevalence of adverse childhood experiences in secure children's home admissions', *Child Youth Care Forum*.

May, R. (1998) *Power and Innocence*, London: W.W. Norton and Company.

McAdams, D.P. (1995) 'What do we know when we know a person?', *Journal of Personality*, 63:363–396.

McAdams, D.P. and McLean, K.C. (2013) 'Narrative identity', *Current Directions in Psychological Science*, 22(3):233–238.

McAdams, D.P. and Pals, J.L. (2006) 'A new Big Five: fundamental principles for an integrative science of personality', *American Psychologist*, 61:204–217.

McCartan, K.F. (2020) *Trauma-informed Practice,* Academic Insights 2020/05, Manchester: HM Inspectorate of Probation.

Meek, R. (2018) *A Sporting Change: An Independent Review of Sport in Youth and Adult Prisons*, London: Ministry of Justice.

Mehta, M.A., Golembo, N.I., Nosarti, C., Colvert, E., Mota, A. and Williams, S.C.R., et al (2009) 'Amygdala, hippocampal and corpus callosum size following severe early institutional deprivation: the English and Romanian Adoptees Study pilot', *Journal of Child Psychology and Psychiatry*, 50(8):943–951.

Meltzer, H., Doos, L., Vostanis, P., Ford, T. and Goodman, R. (2009) 'The mental health of children who witness domestic violence', *Child and Family Social Work*, 14:491–501.

Mendoza, K. and Bradley, L. (2021) 'A model of storytelling: working with traumatically abused children', *Journal of Mental Health Counseling*, 1–18.

Mercy, J.A., Butchart, A., Farrington, D. and Cerdá, M. (2002) 'Youth violence', in E.G. Krug, L.L. Dahlberg, J.A. Mercy, A.B. Zwi and R. Lozano (eds) *World Report on Violence and Health*, Geneva: World Health Organization.

Mersky, J.P., Lee, C.T.P. and Gilbert, R.M. (2019) 'Client and provider discomfort with an adverse childhood experiences survey', *American Journal of Preventive Medicine*, 57(2):51–58.

Ministry of Housing, Communities and Local Government (2019) *The English Indices of Deprivation 2019,* London: Ministry of Housing, Communities and Local Government.

Ministry of Justice (2020) *Knife and Offensive Weapon Sentencing Statistics, England and Wales: Year ending September 2019*, London: Ministry of Justice.

Ministry of Justice and Youth Justice Board (2019) *Standards for Children in the Youth Justice System 2019*, London: Youth Justice Board.

Minsky, R. (1998) *Psychoanalysis and Culture: Contemporary States of Mind*, Cambridge: Polity.

Moylan, C.A., Herrenkohl, T.I., Sousa, C., Tajima, E.A., Herrenkohl, R.C. and Russo, M.J. (2010) 'The effects of child abuse and exposure to domestic violence on adolescent internalizing and externalizing behavior problems', *Journal of Family Violence*, 25:53–63.

Overstreet, S. and Braun, S. (2000) 'Exposure to community violence and post-traumatic stress symptoms: mediating factors', *The American Journal of Orthopsychiatry*, 70(2):263–271.

Ozer, E.J. (2016) 'Youth-led participatory action research', in L. Jason and D. Glenwick (eds) *Handbook of Methodological Approaches to Community-Based Research: Qualitative, Quantitative and Mixed Methods*, New York: Oxford University Press.

Palombo, D.J., McKinnon, M.C., McIntosh, A.R., Anderson, A.K., Todd, R.M. and Levine B. (2016) 'The neural correlates of memory for a life-threatening event: an fMRI study of passengers from flight AT236', *Clin Psychol Sci*, 4(2):312–319.

Parsons, M. (2009) 'The roots of violence: theory and implications for technique with children and adolescents', in M. Lanyado and A. Horne (eds) *The Handbook of Child and Adolescent Psychotherapy. Psychoanalytic Approaches* (Second edition), Abingdon: Routledge.

Perera, J. (2020) *How Black Working-Class Youth are Criminalised and Excluded in the English School System: A London Case Study*. London: Institute of Race Relations.

Perez, N.M., Jennings, W.G. and Baglivio, M.T. (2018) 'A path to serious, violent, chronic delinquency: the harmful aftermath of adverse childhood experiences', *Crime and Delinquency*, 64(1):3–25.

Perry, B.D. and Szalavitz, M. (2007) *The Boy who was Raised as a Dog: What Traumatized Children Can Teach Us About Loss, Love and Healing,* New York: Basic Books.

Prilleltensky, I. (2020) 'Mattering at the intersection of psychology, philosophy, and politics', *American Journal of Community Psychology*, 65(1–2):16–34.

Reuben, A., Moffitt, T.E., Caspi, A., Belsky, D.W., Harrington, H. and Schroeder, F., et al (2016) 'Lest we forget: comparing retrospective and prospective assessments of adverse childhood experiences in the prediction of adult health', *Journal of Child Psychology and Psychiatry,* 57(10):1103–1112.

Riggs, D. and Palasinski, M. (2011) 'Tackling knife violence. Young men view things differently', *British Medical Journal,* 342:d2903.

Rogers, A. and Budd, M. (2015) 'Developing safe and strong foundations: the DART framework', in A. Rogers, J. Harvey and H. Law (eds) *Young People in Forensic Mental Health Settings: Psychological Thinking and Practice*, London: Palgrave.

Ryan, T. and Mitchell, P. (2011) 'A collaborative approach to meeting the needs of adolescent offenders with complex needs in custodial settings: an 18-month cohort study', *Journal of Forensic Psychiatry and Psychology*, 22(3):437–54.

Salzburg Global Seminar (2022) Global Innovations on Youth Violence, Safety and Justice, https://reports.salzburgglobal.org/youth-justice

SAMHSA (2014) *SAMHSA's Concept of Trauma and Guidance for a Trauma-Informed Approach*, Substance Abuse and Mental Health Services Administration Trauma and Justice Strategic Initiative.

Schaefer, C.E. (ed) (2011) *Foundations of Play Therapy*, Hoboken: John Wiley and Sons.

Siegel, D.J. (2001) 'Toward an interpersonal neurobiology of the developing mind: attachment relationships, "mindsight" and neural integration', *Infant Mental Health Journal*, 22(1–2):67–94.

Sitnick, S.L., Shaw, D.S., Weaver, C.M., Shelleby, E.C., Choe, D.E. and Reuben, J.D., et al (2017) 'Early childhood predictors of severe youth violence in low-income male adolescents', *Child Development*, 88(1):27–40.

Skar, A.M.S., Ormhaug, S.M. and Jensen, T.K. (2019) 'Reported levels of upset in youth after routine trauma screening at mental health clinics', *JAMA Network Open,* 2(5):194003–194003.

Skuse, T. and Matthew, J. (2015) 'The trauma recovery model: sequencing youth justice interventions for young people with complex needs', *Prison Service Journal*, 220:16–25.

Smithson, H. and Jones, A. (2021) 'Co-creating youth justice practice with young people: tackling power dynamics and enabling transformative action', *Children and Society*, 35(3):348–362.

Smithson H., Gray, P. and Jones, A. (2021) '"They really should start listening to you": the benefits and challenges of co-producing a participatory framework of youth justice practice', *Youth Justice*, 21(3):321–337.

Smithson, H., Ralphs, R. and Williams, P. (2013) 'Used and abused: the problematic usage of gang terminology in the United Kingdom and its implications for ethnic minority youth', *British Journal of Criminology*, 53(1):113–128.

Stern, D.N. (1985) 'Affect attunement', *Frontiers of Infant Psychiatry*, 2.

Stubley, J. (2022a) 'Complex trauma: the initial consultation', in J. Stubley and L. Young (eds) *Complex Trauma: The Tavistock Model*, Abingdon: Routledge.

Stubley, J. (2022b) 'The Tavistock Trauma Service', in J. Stubley and L. Young (eds) *Complex Trauma: The Tavistock Model*, Abingdon: Routledge.

Stubley, J. and Young, L. (eds) (2022) *Complex Trauma: The Tavistock Model*, Abingdon: Routledge.

Taylor, J., Shostak, L., Rogers, A. and Mitchell, P. (2018) 'Rethinking mental health provision in the secure estate for children and young people: a framework for integrated care (SECURE STAIRS)', *Safer Communities,* 17(4):193–201.

Teicher, M.H. (2002) 'Scars that won't heal: the neurobiology of child abuse', *Scientific American*, 286(3):68–85.

Thomas, H.E. (1995) 'Experiencing a shame response as a precursor to violence', *Bulletin American Academy Psychiatry Law,* 23(4):587–593.

Tiratelli, M., Quinton, P. and Bradford, B. (2018) 'Does stop and search deter crime? Evidence from ten years of London-wide data', *The British Journal of Criminology,* 58(5):1212–1231.

Traynor, P. (2016) 'Closing the "Security Gap": Young people, "street life" and knife crime', PhD thesis, Leeds: University of Leeds.

Turner, D., Wolf, A.J., Barra, S., Muller, M., Hertz, P.G. and Huss, M., et al (2021) 'The association between adverse childhood experiences and mental health problems in young offenders', *European Child and Adolescent Psychiatry*, 30:1195–1207.

Van der Kolk, B. (2014) *The Body Keeps the Score: Mind, Brain and Body in the Transformation of Trauma*, New York: Penguin.

Vaughan, C. (2014) 'Participatory research with youth: idealising safe social spaces or building transformative links in difficult environments?', *Journal of Health Psychology,* 19(1):184–192.

Vaughn, M.G., Salas-Wright, C.P., DeLisi, M. and Perron, B. (2014) 'Correlates of traumatic brain injury among juvenile offenders: a multi-site study', *Criminal Behaviour and Mental Health*, 24(3):188–203.

Walsh, D., McCartney, G., Smith, M. and Armour, G. (2019) 'Relationship between childhood socioeconomic position and adverse childhood experiences (ACEs): a systematic review', *Journal of Epidemiology and Community Health*, 73:1087–1093.

Weaver, C.M., Borkowski, J.G. and Whitman, T.L. (2008) 'Violence breeds violence: childhood exposure and adolescent conduct problems', *Journal of Community Psychology*, 36(1):96–112.

Welfare, H. and Hollin, C. (2012) 'Involvement in extreme violence and violence-related trauma: a review with relevance to young people in custody', *Legal and Criminological Psychology*, 17:89–104.

Widom, C.S. (1989) 'The cycle of violence', *Science*, 244(4901):160–166.

Wilkinson, D. (2001) 'Violent events and social identity: specifying the relationship between respect and masculinity in inner-city youth violence', *Sociological Studies of Children and Youth*, 8:231–265.

Williams, P. (2015) 'Criminalising the other: challenging the race–gang nexus', *Race and Class*, 56(3):18–35.

Williams, W.H., Chitsabesan, P., Fazel, S., McMillan, T., Hughes, N., Parsonage, M. and Tonks, J. (2018) 'Traumatic brain injury: a potential cause of violent crime?', *Lancet Psychiatry*, 5(10):836–844.

Wolff, K.T., Baglivio, M.T., Klein, H.J., Piquero, A.R., DeLisi, M. and Howell, J.C. (2020) 'Adverse Childhood Experiences (ACEs) and gang involvement among juvenile offenders: assessing the mediation effects of substance use and temperament deficits', *Youth Violence and Juvenile Justice*, 18(1):24–53.

World Health Organization (2015) *Preventing Youth Violence: An Overview of the Evidence*, Geneva: World Health Organization.

World Health Organization (2022) *ICD-11 – International Classification of Diseases* 11th Revision, www.who.int/standards/classifications/classification-of-diseases

Wright, S., Liddle, M. and Goodfellow, P. (2016) *Developing Trauma-Informed Resettlement for Young Custody Leavers. A Practitioner's Guide*, London: Nacro.

Yakeley, J. (2018) 'Psychodynamic approaches to violence', *BJPsych Advances*, 24(2):83–92.

Yakeley, J. and Adshead, G. (2013) 'Locks, keys, and security of mind: Psychodynamic approaches to forensic psychiatry', *Journal of the American Academy of Psychiatry and the Law*, 41:38–45.

Youth Justice Board (2014) *AssetPlus Model Document*, London: Youth Justice Board.

Youth Justice Board (2020) *Business Plan 2020/21*, London: Youth Justice Board.

Youth Justice Board (2021) *Strategic Plan 2021–2024*, London: Youth Justice Board.

Youth Justice Board and Ministry of Justice (2022) *Youth Justice Statistics 2020/21 England and Wales*, London: Ministry of Justice.

Index

References to figures appear in *italic* type; those in **bold** type refer to tables. References to endnotes show both the page number and the note number (109n5).

A

adolescent behaviour 81
adverse childhood experiences (ACEs) 3, 4, 6–8, 11, 12–18, 21, 42, 84, 85, 100–102, 104
  assessment tool 22–26, 66–68
  participatory workshops 29–40
  prevalence of 54–58
  qualitative interviews 27–29
  and serious youth violence 69–83
  types of *14*, 58–66
'affect attunement' 82
Anda, R.F. 76
antisocial behaviour 10
Asmussen, K. 56, 63
AssetPlus 68
attachment theory 81–83
attention deficit hyperactivity disorder (ADHD) 17, 74
autism spectrum disorder (ASD) 17
automatic anxiety 77

B

Baglivio, M.T. 16
behavioural disturbances 70
Billingham, L. 11
Black, Asian and minority ethnic (BAME) young people 43, 104, 105
Black Lives Matter movement 104
The Body Keeps the Score (Van der Kolk) 75
Boswell, G. 56, 60, 62, 63
Bowlby, J. 81, 82

Braga, T. 16
Business Plan 2020/21 20

C

caregiver relationship 81
Case, S. 20
Centers for Disease Control and Prevention 12
Child and Adolescent Mental Health Services (CAMHS) 109n5
Child and Adolescent Trauma Screen 24
child criminal exploitation (CCE) 17, 74, 79
Child First approach 87, 101
Child First youth justice system 92
childhood adversity 1, 22, 56, 69
clinical psychotherapeutic support 100
Comic Relief 32
community and neighbourhood factors 10
'complex trauma' 70
consequential thinking, lack of 53
Craig, J.M. 16
'creative therapy' 109n6
Crime Survey for England and Wales (CSEW) 2, 11

D

Dent–Brown, K. 6
destructive behaviour 82
domestic violence 10, 15, 63, 64, 77
'double childhood trauma' 15
'drama therapy' 109n6

E

Early Intervention Foundation 13
effective trauma-informed
   practice 94
*Eleventh Revision of The International
   Classification of Diseases* 70
Elliott, G. 80
'emotional abuse' 15, 61
'emotional neglect' 61
emotional trauma 13
emotional well-being 72
Enhanced Case Management
   project 94

F

'familial substance use' 61
Felitti, V.J. 6
'fight-or-flight' hormones 8
fight-or-flight response 75, 76
first-time entrants (FTEs) 42
Fonagy, P. 83
forensic psychotherapy 103
Fox, B. 15, 71

G

Garland, C. 77, 90
Gilligan, J. 102

H

Haines, K. 20
Hawkins, J.D. 9, 10
Herman, J.L. 70
hippocampus 8

I

industrial revolution 1
innovative methodology 4
interpersonal violence 11
Irwin-Rogers, K. 11

J

Jacobson, J. 56
justice-involved young people,
   narrative interviews with 27–29

K

Kirby, A. 75
Knife Crime Prevention Orders 3,
   11, 106n8

L

Lemma, A. 97
Levinson, A. 83
life narratives 28

M

Maas, C. 16, 62
Manchester Youth Justice
   Service 25–27, 30, 96
Martin, A. 13, 54, 55, 58
May, Theresa 11
McAdams Life Story Approach 6
McAdams Life Story Interview 28
mental health problems 15, 56, 71
Mersky, J.P. 24
mixed-methods approach 21
'multi-pronged, multiagency'
   approach 94

N

narrative identity 28
neurodevelopmental disorders
   (NDDs) 7, 17, 74
neurodivergence 17
neuroendocrine systems 76
NVivo 107n3

P

Palombo, D.J. 76
'parental separation/loss' 60
Parsons, M. 82
participatory workshops 29
   delivering workshops 34–35
   designing workshops 30–32
   emergent themes from
      workshops 35–40
   six-part stories 35
   workshop participants 32–34
Participatory Youth Practice
   (PYP) 20, 30, 103

peer-related factors 10
Photovoice 38
physical abuse 62, 63, 73, 89
Police, Crime, Sentencing and
  Courts Act 2022 105
posttraumatic stress disorder
  (PTSD) 70
poverty 1, 10
Prison Reform Trust 15, 63
'problematic behaviours' 69
psychological homeostasis 82
psychotherapeutic formulation 96
psychotherapeutic modality 81

S

SAMHSA 84, 85, 87, 94
Section 18 of the Offences Against
  the Person Act 1861 107n4
Section 53 of the Children and
  Young Persons Act 1933 107n7
'secure base' 82
self-directed violence 16
semi-structured interviews 22, 27
Serious Violence Reduction
  Orders 11, 107n2
Serious Violence Strategy 11
'Serious Violence Summit' 3, 11
Serious Violence Taskforce 3
serious youth violence (SYV) 1–5,
  7–12, 21, 27, 30, 34, 40, 60, 66,
  84, 101, 103–105
  adverse childhood experiences
    and 69–83
  level and type of 41–43
  reasons for 43–48
  reasons for carrying a knife 48–53
signal anxiety 77
6-Part Story Method (6PSM) 6,
  30, 34, 35
Skar, A.M.S. 24
social control theory 16
socio-economic deprivation 65
Stern, D.N. 82
strengths-based model 87
Stubley, J. 92, 96
subsequent behaviour 82

Substance Abuse and Mental
  Health Services Administration
  (SAMHSA) 18
suffragette movement 1

T

therapeutic modalities 96
trauma-informed approach 5, 8,
  19, 100, 101
  barriers to delivering 88–94
  implementing 94–99
  strengths of 84–87
trauma-informed care 85
trauma-informed practice 17–19,
  81, 100, 102–104, 108n3
trauma-informed service 100
traumatic brain injury (TBI) 7, 17,
  18, 75
traumatic childhood
  memories 102
traumatic events 105

U

Unit Award Scheme 32, 108n7

V

Van der Kolk, B. 76
  The Body Keeps the Score 75
Vaughn, M.G. 18
ventromedial prefrontal cortex 8
violence 11
  domestic 10, 15, 63, 64, 77
  interpersonal 11
  self-directed 16
  young people's involvement in 39
Violence Reduction Units 3, 11
violent behaviour 102
violent victimization 18, 63

W

Wang, M. 6
Williams, W.H. 18
witnessed domestic violence 63,
  64, 72, 73

Wolff, K.T. 79
workshops
  delivering 34–35
  designing 30–32
  emergent themes from 35–40
  participants 32–34
*World Report on Violence
  and Health* 9

Y

Young, L. 92, 97
young people's involvement in
  violence **39**

Youth Endowment Fund (YEF) 3,
  11, 106n1, 106n7
Youth Justice Board 20, 25,
  106n4, 108n2
*Youth Justice Statistics
  2020/21* 42
youth justice system 100,
  103, 105
youth justice workers 101
  interviews with 27
youth participation 19–20
Youth Violence Commission 3,
  11, 65, 104